INFORMATION SECURITY: CONTEMPORARY CASES

MARIE A. WRIGHT, PhD

Western Connecticut State University

JOHN S. KAKALIK, PhD

Western Connecticut State University

JONES AND BARTLETT PUBLISHERS

Sudbury, Massachusetts

BOSTON   TORONTO   LONDON   SINGAPORE

World Headquarters

Jones and Bartlett Publishers	Jones and Bartlett Publishers	Jones and Bartlett Publishers
40 Tall Pine Drive	Canada	International
Sudbury, MA 01776	6339 Ormindale Way	Barb House, Barb Mews
978-443-5000	Mississauga, Ontario L5V 1J2	London W6 7PA
info@jbpub.com	CANADA	UK
www.jbpub.com		

Jones and Bartlett's books and products are available through most bookstores and online book-sellers. To contact Jones and Bartlett Publishers directly, call 800-832-0034, fax 978-443-8000, or visit our website www.jbpub.com.

Substantial discounts on bulk quantities of Jones and Bartlett's publications are available to cor-porations, professional associations, and other qualified organizations. For details and specific discount information, contact the special sales department at Jones and Bartlett via the above contact information or send an email to specialsales@jbpub.com.

Library of Congress Cataloging-in-Publication Data
Wright, Marie A.
  Information security : contemporary cases / Marie A. Wright, John S. Kakalik.
    p. cm.
  Includes bibliographical references and index.
  ISBN 0-7637-3819-0 (pbk.)
  1. Computer security—Case studies. 2. Computer networks—Security measures—Case studies.
I. Kakalik, John S. II. Title.
  QA76.9.A25W75 2006
  005.8—dc22
                              2005036449
6048

Production Credits
Acquisitions Editor: Tim Anderson
Production Director: Amy Rose
Editorial Assistant: Kate Koch
Production Editor: Tracey Chapman
Marketing Manager: Andrea DeFronzo
Vice President of Manufacturing and Inventory Control: Therese Connell
Composition: Arlene Apone
Cover Design: Kristin E. Ohlin
Cover Image: © EyeWire, Inc.
Printing and Binding: Malloy, Inc.
Cover Printing: Malloy, Inc.

Printed in the United States of America
10 09 08 07 06   10 9 8 7 6 5 4 3 2 1

DEDICATION

In Memory of Our Fathers:

Arthur Wright
Mitti Kakalik

To Our Mothers:

Ethel Wright
Veronica Kakalik

PREFACE

Information security education is a top national priority. Since September 11, 2001, the importance of information security education has been repeatedly emphasized by numerous entities, including the White House, the Department of Homeland Security (DHS), the Federal Bureau of Investigation (FBI), the National Security Agency (NSA), the North American Aerospace Defense Command (NORAD), the U.S. Northern Command (USNORTHCOM), and Congress. Yet, despite the increased number of information security courses and programs in higher education, many college graduates are not prepared to work in the profession because of inadequate preparation in the practical aspects of information security. Although it is well known that learning is enhanced when theory and practice are integrated, students often have difficulty relating classroom material to the practical working environment. The absence of any casebooks in information security has compounded the challenge faced by information security educators and potential employers. *Information Security: Contemporary Cases* is intended to fill this void.

   Information Security: Contemporary Cases addresses information security concepts in realistic scenarios. This book consists of a diverse series of substantive, in-depth case studies. Each case focuses on a different aspect of information security addressed by a real organization. The case studies are drawn from personally obtained information. The situations are real and the organizations are identified by name. Each case study is covered in sufficient breadth and depth to enable students to understand the organization and its security scenario. By providing students with real information security situations encountered in a variety of organizations, this book helps students to develop the practical understanding needed to cope effectively with the responsibilities of the profession.

Summary Description of Case Studies

The first case study, "Protecting Employee Data," describes the systems, processes, and formal arrangements that have been implemented by Kraft Foods Inc. to ensure the security and privacy of its employees' personal data.

   The second case study, "Integrating IT and Physical Security," describes how two national crises triggered immediate changes in the physical security and process security controls at Advo, Inc. It focuses on the treatment of information technology and physical security as interconnected components of Advo Inc.'s evolving security infrastructure.

   The third case study, "Contingency Planning," describes the disaster planning initiatives, education and training programs, clinical strategies, and logistical solutions developed by the Yale New Haven Center for Emergency Preparedness and Disaster Response.

   The fourth case study, "The Embedded Security Subsystem," addresses the need for trusted hardware. It describes an integrated security chip developed by IBM, and it explains the means by which this chip can provide strong user authentication and system integrity.

The fifth case study, "Automating Compliance with Federal Information Security Requirements," describes how SRA International, Inc. has automated the process of complying with federal government information security regulations through the use of its Web-based risk assessment software.

The sixth case study, "Tracking a Computer Intruder," describes the methods and processes used by the FBI New Haven field office to locate an intruder who hacked into a Connecticut e-commerce company's computer system.

The seventh case study, "Developing and Implementing a Successful Information Security Awareness Program," describes the information security awareness program at Aetna. It explains the development and implementation processes, and it describes the content of the program.

Case Structure

All case studies have been developed to provide a thorough and meaningful application of information security concepts. Each case study contains the following:

- *Overview:* a brief synopsis of the case topic, the organization, and the major concepts addressed in the case study;
- *Background:* a description of the organization, including its mission, history, size, and structure, which provides the foundation and context for the case study;
- *Information Security Subject Treatment:* an in-depth description of the case study topic and related information security concepts;
- *Final Comments:* concluding remarks that summarize the current status of the organization and outline future directions;
- *Endnotes:* a list of resources used in developing the case study;

■ *Case Study Questions:* a list of ten questions intended to measure student understanding and foster critical thinking. Some of the solutions require computer work, some require further exploration and research, and all require thought;

■ *Key Terms:* a list of key terms used in the case study, along with their definitions; and

■ *Appendices:* included as needed in some case studies to provide additional coverage of case-related information security topics.

Intended Audience

This book is intended for use in Information Security and Information Assurance courses at the undergraduate or at the first-year master's level. Because the case studies can be covered in greater or lesser depth, this book can be used as a supplement or as a stand-alone text. As a supplement, the cases provide a variety of realistic and practical examples that clarify and reinforce the information security concepts addressed in Information Systems, Computer Science, and Justice and Law courses. As a stand-alone text, the case studies are sufficient in number and depth for an Information Security or Information Assurance seminar class.

Instructor's Manual

The accompanying instructor's manual includes the following:

■ a description of how each case study fits with some of the leading information security textbooks currently on the market;

■ an overview and synopsis of each case study;

■ suggested, detailed answers to the case study questions;

■ suggestions for expanding each case study for further depth or application; and

■ an epilogue, providing updates on events that occurred after specific case studies were written.

About the Authors

Marie A. Wright, PhD, is a professor of Management Information Systems at Western Connecticut State University. There, she developed the nation's first undergraduate course in information systems security and led the implementation of the nation's first interdisciplinary undergraduate program in information security management within a school of business. She received her PhD in Information and Control Systems from the University of Massachusetts at Amherst and has been actively involved in the field of information systems security and information assurance for more than fifteen years. In addition to authoring numerous articles and book chapters, she is a frequent speaker at information security conferences, colloquia, and symposia. She also participates in many professional information security organizations.

John S. Kakalik, PhD, is the co-chair of the Marketing Department and a full-time faculty member at Western Connecticut State University. He received his PhD in Marketing from Michigan State University and has been a member of the faculties at the University of Maine at Orono and the University of New Haven, where he was also the Associate Dean of the School of Business Administration. He has been a consultant to General Motors, the Federal Trade Commission, General Electric, and various state and regional businesses and law firms. His research interests focus on consumer privacy and the protection of sensitive information, and he has contributed to the information systems security and information assurance profession through the publication of a number of articles.

Acknowledgments

This book would not have been possible without the participation of the remarkable individuals who willingly shared their knowledge, enthusiasm, and expertise with us as we developed these case studies. We are grateful to the following individuals and organizations:

Kraft Foods Inc., Northfield, IL
    Mr. Mark Ready—Director, Human Resources Technology and Information
    Mr. Mike Kelly—Associate Director, Human Resources Technology and Information
    Mr. David Aird—Corporate Account Management, Global Information Systems
    Ms. Debra Byars—Director, Global Information Risk Management

Advo, Inc., Windsor, CT
    Mr. Philip McMurray—Director, IT Security and Enterprise Architecture
    Mr. Frank LaMorte—Director of Corporate Security

Yale New Haven Health, New Haven, CT
    Mr. Christopher Cannon—Director, Center for Emergency Preparedness and Disaster Response

IBM Watson Research Center, Hawthorne, NY
    Dr. David Safford—Manager, Global Security Analysis Lab

SRA International, Inc., Arlington, VA
    Mr. Michael Jacobs—Vice President and Director, Cyber and National Security Program
    Mr. William Bell—Director, Information Assurance Division
    Mr. Steven Newburg-Rinn—Principal and Director, Civil Government IA Solutions
    Mr. Daniel VanBelleghem, Jr.—Technical Director, Information Assurance Group

FBI New Haven Field Office, New Haven, CT
> The Special Agents and the Supervisory Special Agent (Individual names have been withheld at their request for anonymity)

Aetna, Hartford, CT
> Ms. Donna Richmond—Security Advisor, Information Security Policy and Practices

We are grateful to Dr. James W. Schmotter, President of Western Connecticut State University, for his considerable support and assistance. We appreciate the case study reviews and commentary provided by the students in Western Connecticut State University's "Information Systems Security" classes. We also thank April Boudreau for her assistance. Finally, we extend our thanks to the staff at Jones and Bartlett Publishers, especially Tim Anderson, Jenny Bagdigian, Tracey Chapman, Kate Koch, and Kristin Rayla.

CONTENTS

KRAFT FOODS INC.:

PROTECTING EMPLOYEE DATA

All companies are expected to protect the confidentiality and integrity of their employees' data. This means that all companies must implement the controls needed to effectively balance the nature of the data against the amount of risk involved in accessing, processing, storing, and transmitting that data. For global a company such as Kraft Foods Inc., the controls also must ensure compliance with the data privacy regulations that exist in all countries in which it operates.

This case study describes the systems, processes, and formal arrangements that have been implemented by Kraft Foods Inc., to ensure the security and privacy of its employees' personal data. To provide necessary background information, the case study begins with an overview of Kraft Foods Inc., its history and structure, and summarizes key aspects of the European Union Directive on the Protection of Personal Data.

Kraft Foods Inc.

Kraft Foods Inc., is the largest food and beverage company in North America and it is the second largest food and beverage company in the world. The company's 2004 reported net earnings were $2.665 billion on net revenues of $32.168 billion. As of December 31, 2004, the Company employed approximately 98,000 people worldwide.[1]

Kraft manufactures and sells its branded cheese, dairy products, snacks, convenient meals, grocery products and beverages in the United States, Canada, Europe, the Middle East, Africa, Latin America, and Asia Pacific. Its products are sold in more than 155 countries. Almost all American households (99.6%) have purchased Kraft products.[1] Table 1-1 shows the principal brands sold in the United States and Canada. Table 1-2 shows the principal brands sold in Europe, the Middle East, Africa, Latin America, and Asia Pacific.

Kraft operates 192 manufacturing and processing facilities worldwide. Eighty-seven of those facilities are in North America (United States and Canada) and 105 facilities are located in forty-four countries throughout Europe, the Middle East, Africa, Latin America, and Asia Pacific. Kraft also operates 331 distribution centers and depots in North America and an additional twenty-five distribution centers in nine countries.[1]

Its brands, considered to be the best in the food business, hold the number one market share position in twenty-one product categories, including cheese, coffee, powdered soft drinks, cookies, crackers, convenient meals, salad dressings, refrigerated ready-to-eat desserts, steak sauce and marinades, and snack nuts.[2]

History

The Northfield, Illinois–based company began in 1903, when James L. Kraft began selling cheese from a horse-drawn wagon to grocers in Chicago, Illinois. Within a few years, Kraft was distributing more than

TABLE 1-1 Principal Brands Sold in the United States and Canada (Kraft North America Commercial)

Cheese and dairy: *Kraft* and *Cracker Barrel* natural cheeses; *Philadelphia* cream cheese; *Kraft* and *Velveeta* process cheeses; *Kraft* grated cheeses; *Cheez Whiz* process cheese sauce; *Easy Cheese* aerosol cheese spread; and *Knudsen* and *Breakstone's* cottage cheese and sour cream.

Snacks: *Oreo, Chips Ahoy!, Newtons, Peak Freans, Nilla, Nutter Butter, Stella D'Oro* and *SnackWell's* cookies; *Ritz, Premium, Triscuit, Wheat Thins, Cheese Nips, Better Cheddars, Honey Maid Grahams,* and *Teddy Grahams* crackers; *Planters* nuts and salted snacks; *Terry's* and *Toblerone* chocolate confectionery products; *Handi-Snacks* two-compartment snacks; *Fun Fruits* sugar confectionery products; and *Balance* nutrition and energy snacks.

Convenient meals: *DiGiorno, Tombstone, Jack's, California Pizza Kitchen* (under license), and *Delissio* frozen pizzas; *Kraft* macaroni & cheese dinners; *Taco Bell Home Originals* meal kits (under license); *Lunchables* lunch combinations; *Oscar Mayer* and *Louis Rich* cold cuts, hot dogs, and bacon; *Boca* soy-based meat alternatives; *Stove Top* stuffing mix; and *Minute* rice.

Grocery: *Cool Whip* frozen whipped topping; *Back to Nature* products; *Post* ready-to-eat cereals; *Cream of Wheat* and *Cream of Rice* hot cereals; *Kraft* peanut butter; *Kraft* and *Miracle Whip* spoonable dressings; *Kraft* salad dressings; *A1* steak sauce; *Kraft* and *Bull's-Eye* barbecue sauces; *Grey Poupon* premium mustards; *Shake 'N Bake* coatings; *Jell-O* dry packaged desserts and refrigerated gelatin and pudding snacks; *Handi-Snacks* shelf-stable pudding snacks; *Del Monte* and *Aylmer* canned fruits and vegetables; and *Milk-Bone* pet snacks.

Beverages: *Maxwell House, General Foods International Coffees, Starbucks* (under license), *Yuban, Seattle's Best* (under license), *Sanka, Nabob,* and *Gevalia* coffees; *Capri Sun* (under license), *Tang, Kool-Aid,* and *Crystal Light* aseptic juice drinks; *Kool-Aid, Tang, Crystal Light,* and *Country Time* powdered beverages; *Veryfine* juices; *Tazo* teas (under license); and *Fruit$_2$O* water.

Source: U.S. Securities and Exchange Commission, Form 10-K, Annual Report for the Year Ended December 31, 2004, Altria Group, Inc. Available: http://www.altria.com/investors/02_07_01_secFilingData.asp?showHeader=True & URL=http://ccbn.10kwizard.com/xml/contents.xml?ipage=3335007~repo=tenk

TABLE 1-2 Principal Brands Sold in Europe, the Middle East, Africa, Latin America, and Asia Pacific (Kraft International Commercial)

Cheese and dairy: *Philadelphia* cream cheese; *Sottilette, Kraft, Dairylea, Osella,* and *El Caserío* cheeses; *Kraft* and *Eden* process cheeses; and *Cheez Whiz* process cheese spread.

Snacks: *Milka, Suchard, Côte d'Or, Marabou, Toblerone, Freia, Terry's, Daim, Figaro, Korona, Poiana, Prince Polo, Alpen Gold, Siesta, Pokrov, Lacta,* and *Gallito* chocolate confectionery products; *Estrella, Maarud, Cipso,* and *Lux* salted snacks; and *Oreo, Chips Ahoy!, Ritz, Terrabusi, Club Social, Cerealitas, Trakinas,* and *Lucky* biscuits.

Convenient meals: *Lunchables* lunch combinations; *Kraft* macaroni & cheese dinners; *Kraft* and *Mirácoli* pasta dinners and sauces; and *Simmenthal* canned meats.

Grocery: *Kraft* spoonable and pourable salad dressings; *Miracle Whip* spoonable dressings; *Royal* dry packaged desserts; *Kraft* and *ETA* peanut butters; and *Vegemite* yeast spread.

Beverages: *Jacobs, Gevalia, Carte Noire, Jacques Vabre, Kaffee HAG, Grand' Mère, Kenco, Saimaza, Maxim, Maxwell House, Dadak, Onko, Samar, Tassimo,* and *Nova Brasilia* coffees; *Suchard Express, O'Boy,* and *Kaba* chocolate drinks; *Tang, Clight, Kool-Aid, Royal, Verao, Fresh, Frisco, Q-Refres-Ko,* and *Ki-Suco* powdered beverages; *Maguary* juice concentrate and ready-to-drink beverages; and *Capri Sun* aseptic juice drinks (under license).

Source: U.S. Securities and Exchange Commission, Form 10-K, Annual Report for the Year Ended December 31, 2004, Altria Group, Inc. Available: http://www.altria.com/investors/02_07_01_secFilingData.asp?showHeader=True & URL=http://ccbn.10kwizard.com/xml/contents.xml?ipage=3335007~repo=tenk.

thirty varieties of cheese to grocers in cities and towns throughout the United States. In 1914, the Kraft Cheese Company opened its first plant and began processing its own cheese. During the 1920s, Kraft began selling its cheese in Canada, Europe, and Australia. In 1928, it acquired the Phenix Cheese Company, maker of *Philadelphia* brand cream cheese.

Over the next two decades, Kraft introduced a number of new products, including *Velveeta* pasteurized process cheese, *Miracle Whip* salad dressing, and *Kraft* macaroni and cheese dinner. In 1955, Kraft opened a processing plant in Mexico, making it the first U.S. firm to have process cheese and salad dressing production facilities in Mexico.[3]

In 1988, Kraft was acquired by Philip Morris Companies Inc. Philip Morris had acquired General Foods Corporation in 1985, and with the acquisition of Kraft, Philip Morris became the world's largest consumer products company.

In 1989, the food product divisions of Philip Morris (General Foods and Kraft) were joined to become Kraft General Foods. That same year, Kraft General Foods International was established as a subsidiary of Kraft General Foods. In 1993, Kraft General Foods acquired the U.S. and Canadian ready-to-eat cereal business from RJR Nabisco.[3]

Two years later, Kraft General Foods was reorganized and renamed Kraft Foods Incorporated. North American and international operations were conducted through two subsidiaries of Kraft Foods Inc.: Kraft Foods North America, Inc., and Kraft Foods International, Inc. (formerly Kraft General Foods International). The headquarters for Kraft Foods North America, Inc., was located in Northfield, Illinois, and the headquarters for Kraft Foods International, Inc., was located in Rye Brook, New York.

In 2001, the two subsidiaries were consolidated under Kraft Foods Inc., with its world headquarters located in Northfield, Illinois. Kraft Foods North America, Inc., was renamed Kraft North America Commercial, and Kraft Foods International, Inc., was renamed Kraft International Commercial.

On June 13, 2001, Philip Morris Companies Inc., completed an Initial Public Offering of 280,000,000 shares of Kraft's Class A common stock at a price of $31.00 per share.[2] The transaction was a stock-for-cash exchange, in which the money was used to pay down the debt of Kraft's parent company. Although Kraft Foods Inc., was no longer a wholly owned subsidiary of Philip Morris Companies Inc., Philip Morris continued to retain tight control over Kraft. In 2003, Philip Morris Companies Inc., changed its name to Altria Group, Inc. As of December 31, 2004, Altria Group, Inc., held 98% of the combined voting power of Kraft's outstanding capital stock and 85.4% of the outstanding shares of Kraft's capital stock.[1]

Structure

Kraft's organization is structured along three dimensions: global marketing, geographic commercial units, and global functions. The first dimension, global marketing, is responsible for product category development strategies, and marketing resources and initiatives.[4]

Kraft manages and reports its operating results through two geographic commercial units, which comprise the second dimension. The two commercial units, Kraft North America Commercial (KNAC) and Kraft International Commercial (KIC), are each responsible for determining the marketing and sales programs that best meet the needs of local customers, with profit and loss responsibility for the results. KNAC consists of five U.S. groups and includes thirteen business divisions[4]:

- U.S. Cheese and Dairy;
- U.S. Snacks—Post Division, U.S. Biscuit Division, and U.S. Salted Snacks Division;
- U.S. Convenient Meals—U.S. Meals Division, U.S. Natural and Organic Foods, Oscar Mayer Division, and U.S. Pizza Division;
- U.S. Grocery—U.S. Enhancers Division and U.S. Desserts Division; and
- U.S. Beverages—U.S. Coffee Division and U.S. Refreshment Beverages Division.

In addition, KNAC includes the North America Foodservice Division and Kraft Canada.

KIC includes five geographic regions: (1) Western Europe, (2) Central Europe, (3) Eastern Europe, Middle East, and Africa, (4) Latin America, and (5) Asia Pacific.[4]

The third organizational dimension is formed by Kraft's global functions, which are aligned and linked to global marketing, KNAC and KIC. There are eight global functions:

- *Global Corporate Affairs* is responsible for media relations, marketing communications, internal communications, and charitable contributions worldwide, as well as for coordinating Kraft's corporate responsibility activities and managing the government affairs teams that support the business.[5]
- *Global Finance* handles Kraft's worldwide financial functions, including financial matters with public investors, the board of directors, auditors, and financial regulatory groups.[6]
- *Global Human Resources* is responsible for human resources' services and systems, including employee and labor relations, compensation, benefits, staffing, diversity initiatives, recruitment, and retention.[7]
- *Global Information Systems* is responsible for Kraft's information systems and technology worldwide, including systems analysis and design, project leadership, infrastructure planning and development, information and application architecture framework and standards, life cycle support, evaluating and implementing emerging technologies, and providing security services (e.g., threat and vulnerability analyses, security policies and procedures, risk management, business continuity plans, audit and control management, and access controls).[8]
- *Global Law* is responsible for the company's legal functions worldwide.[9]
- *Global Strategy and Business Development* is responsible for the development of Kraft's corporate business strategies, including merger and acquisition activities around the world.[10]

- *Global Supply Chain* is responsible for procurement, manufacturing and logistics operations and customer service worldwide.[11]
- *Global Technology and Quality* is responsible for all product and packaging development, research, nutrition, quality, food safety and scientific affairs worldwide.[12]

Kraft's Executive Team consists of the leaders of each of the eight global functions, the two geographic commercial units, and global marketing. Each leader reports directly to the Chief Executive Officer. The team is diagrammed in Figure 1-1.

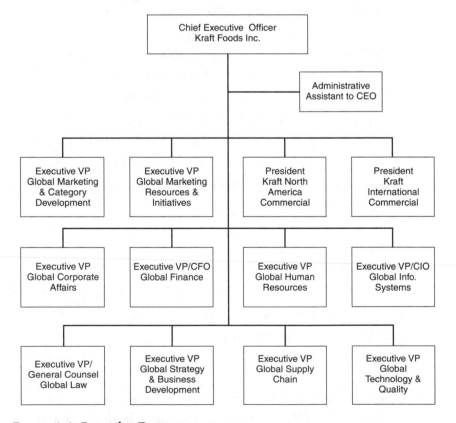

FIGURE 1-1 Executive Team.

Source: Mr. Mark Ready, Director, Human Resources Technology and Information, Kraft Foods Inc., August 1, 2005.

Human Resources Technology and Information

Within the Global Human Resources function, there is a specialized group known as Human Resources Technology and Information (HRT&I). This group works closely with Global Information Systems on Human Resources–related technology projects.[13] HRT&I has numerous responsibilities, among them[8]:

- providing technology and information used to support U.S./Canadian benefits administration, staffing, diversity, work life, training administration, eLearning, compensation processes, payroll, advancement planning (AP), and the Management Appraisal Program;
- providing the human resources (HR) community with information and support for routine and special requests pertaining to metrics, key performance indicators, headcounts, and reorganizations;
- working closely with staffs in different geographic locations to support regional and country-level needs;
- ensuring that all users have the necessary support and tools, such as user training, help desks, and documentation;
- developing and supporting employee and manager self-service software tools and HR intranets;
- identifying opportunities for synergy, improved service, and enhanced employee productivity, such as establishing portals, expert directories, and remote access capabilities; providing training to improve employee computer skills; and developing knowledge management and collaboration tools; and
- ensuring that the systems meet HR and organizational data needs, and spearheading enhancements to system performance, security and reporting.

The HRT&I organizational chart reflects these responsibilities, as shown in Figure 1-2.

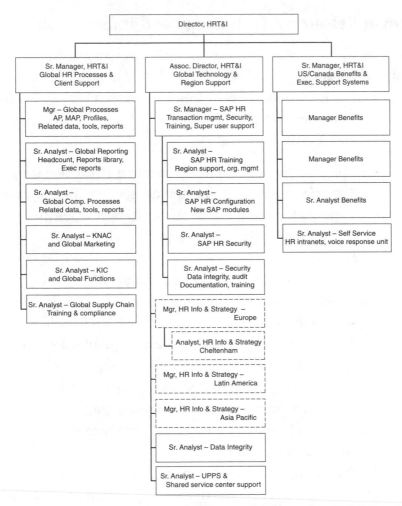

FIGURE 1-2 Human Resources Technology and Information (HRT&I) organizational chart.

Source: Mr. Mark Ready, Director, Human Resources Technology and Information, Kraft Foods Inc., August 1, 2005.

One of HRT&I's ongoing projects concerns the protection of employee data worldwide. Kraft Foods Inc., employs a workforce of approximately 98,000 individuals; more than half (approximately 53,000 employees) are located in sixty-five countries around the world.[1] The company must collect and use personal information from and about its employees so that it can provide compensation and benefits, comply with different tax and labor regulations, and operate effectively and competitively. As a global organization, Kraft must abide by the laws of all countries in which it operates.

Within the European Union (EU) member states, Kraft has operations in Austria, Belgium, Denmark, Finland, France, Germany, Greece, Ireland, Italy, The Netherlands, Portugal, Spain, Sweden, and the United Kingdom. The EU is known for its strict regulations governing the privacy of personal data. Particularly noteworthy is the EU Directive on the Protection of Personal Data.

European Union Directive on the Protection of Personal Data

On October 24, 1995, the EU enacted "Directive 95/46/EC of the European Parliament and of the Council of 24 October 1995 on the protection of individuals with regard to the processing of personal data and on the free movement of such data", more commonly referred to as the *EU Directive on the Protection of Personal Data*. It became effective on October 25, 1998. The Directive has two objectives: to protect individual rights to privacy with respect to the processing of personal data, and to promote the free flow of personal data between EU member states.[14] Defining *personal data* as any information relating to a person, the directive established several requirements for the privacy of this data:

▪ Personal data must be processed fairly and lawfully; collected and processed for explicit and legitimate purposes; relevant and not excessive to the purpose for which the data are collected and processed; accurate; and stored in such a way that allows identification of individuals for no longer than necessary.[14]

▪ Before personal data can be collected, the individual must be informed of the identity of the organization collecting the data, the purposes for which the data are being collected, his or her obligation to provide the data, the recipients of the data, and his or her rights to access the data and correct any inaccuracies.[14]

■ Once collected, personal data may be processed only if the individual has clearly given his or her consent, or if required for contractual or legal reasons, or to protect the interests of the individual, or to perform a task carried out for the public interest.[14]

■ Appropriate technical and organizational controls must be in place to protect personal data from unauthorized access, disclosure, modification, and destruction. The security controls must be commensurate to the nature of the data and to the perceived risks to that data.[14]

To prevent these requirements from being circumvented outside of the EU, the directive allows personal data to be transferred to, or processed by, an organization in a non-EU country only if "an adequate level of protection"[14] can be ensured. For all organizations in the United States and other countries that do business with the EU, this restriction on the transfer and processing of personal data is a critical provision.

With employees in many of the EU member states, Kraft needed to assess the means by which it collected, processed, transmitted, and stored employee data. This meant that it needed to reexamine its HR systems and processes.

Human Resources Systems and Processes

Prior to 2001, Kraft's North American and International operations were conducted through two subsidiaries: Kraft Foods North America, Inc., and Kraft Foods International, Inc. The subsidiaries were treated as two separate entities by Kraft's parent company, Philip Morris, and different HR systems and processes were implemented in each.

In North America, HR transactions were processed through the Unified Personnel and Payroll System (UPPS). Implemented in 1994, this system combined seventeen different HR, payroll, and benefits systems into one HR system for all North American employees. Shortly after UPPS was implemented, the HR processes (employee change and turn-around, performance management, diversity tracking, headcount, AP, and compensation and benefits programs) were harmonized, so that the processes were handled consistently between the divisions. Data standards also were put in place to maintain consistent HR information (e.g., position titles, salary grades, and employment events such as transfers, promotions or departures).[8] A Shared Service Center (SSC) was added in 1995, which provided transactional and customer service support to all salaried and non-union hourly transactions for North American employees.[8] Also, web-based self-service was offered to salaried employees, including the ability to view their paychecks, confirm their personal information, access their credit union accounts, make travel arrangements, and file expense reports.[8]

Internationally, dozens of separate HR systems had been implemented. Processing operations were handled individually by each country, and they were overseen by Kraft Foods International, Inc. In 1999, Philip Morris began to create one HR system for all of its operating companies. It chose an enterprise resource planning system from SAP[15] called SAP HR, and it installed the application software on servers in a secure data center in Wilkes-Barre, Pennsylvania.[16] Work began to convert Kraft's international HR systems to the SAP HR system.

Data Transfer Agreement

To comply with the data privacy requirements specified by the EU directive, a Data Transfer Agreement was legally established between Kraft Foods International, Inc., and all of its operating entities in the EU member states.[17] The Data Transfer Agreement allows certain HR information to be transferred from the Kraft companies in the EU to Kraft Foods Inc., in the United States for the purpose of global HR processing (e.g., AP, benefits administration, compensation administration, and professional development programs). Restrictions on personal data and mandatory data protection principles were clearly specified in the agreement[17]:

- The data that could be transferred were restricted to the employee's identification and contact information (name, address, telephone number, education, and length of time at the company and in the current position), and compensation and benefits data (assessments, performance ratings, development plans, and training);
- Transferred personal data could be disclosed only to the HR personnel who require the data for HR processing, the information technology (IT) personnel who support HR's systems and processes, the functional executives who make HR recommendations and decisions (e.g., employee promotions), and the third-party vendors who provide essential services (e.g., benefits consulting);
- All individuals who had access to personal data were contractually bound to respect the privacy of the data;
- Personal data must be processed, used, and communicated only for specified global HR processes;
- The data would be stored no longer than necessary for HR processing;
- Kraft employees in the EU member states must be informed as to the purposes of the processing;
- Kraft employees in the EU member states have the right to access and correct all data relating to them; and
- Technical and organizational security measures must be enacted by Kraft Foods Inc., in the United States to protect the privacy of personal data.

This last provision had implications that extended beyond the protection of Kraft's EU employee data. Kraft Foods Inc., decided to implement stronger technical and organizational security measures to ensure the privacy of all employee data.

Ensuring the Privacy of Personal Employee Data

In 2002, the position of Chief Information Security Officer (CISO) was created. The CISO occupies an upper level management position, reporting directly to the Executive Vice President/Chief Information Officer in Global Information Systems (see Figure 1-1).

The CISO is responsible for supporting the development, implementation, maintenance, and enhancement of all of Kraft's security-related activities, particularly those that pertain to information technology. The CISO also is responsible for improving the information security culture of the company and ensuring that the overall information security strategy is aligned with Kraft's business needs. To do this, the CISO manages the organization's risk profile, administers user access services, ensures audit compliance, and oversees the security management of all of Kraft's geographic regions (North America, Western Europe, Central Europe, Eastern Europe/Middle East/Africa, Latin America, and Asia Pacific).

Through the CISO, a comprehensive governance structure for information systems was established, a strategy for the future was developed, and stronger data security practices were implemented throughout the organization. Information security policies were developed, including those pertaining to compliance with the Sarbanes-Oxley Act of 2002, business continuity and disaster recovery planning, and backup and recovery processes.[18] Risk mitigation initiatives, including threat and vulnerability analyses, also were instituted. Citicus ONE risk management software[19] is used regularly to conduct risk assessments of individual systems, identify risk factors between systems, record risk remediation activities, monitor the risk status of critical applications, and ensure compliance with existing codes of practice (e.g., BS 7799, ISO/IEC 17799).

Kraft also began to move toward standardized system platforms and architectures as a means of improving data security. Kraft's North American HR system has remained on UPPS (see Figure 1-3). By 2003, all international HR systems at Kraft were converted to the SAP HR system[8] (Figure 1-4).

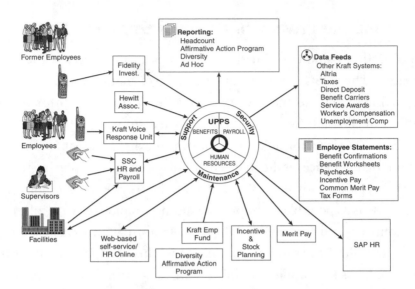

FIGURE 1-3 Unified Personnel and Payroll System (UPPS): North American Human Resources Technology.

Source: Mr. Mark Ready, Director, Human Resources Technology and Information, Kraft Foods Inc., October 19, 2005.

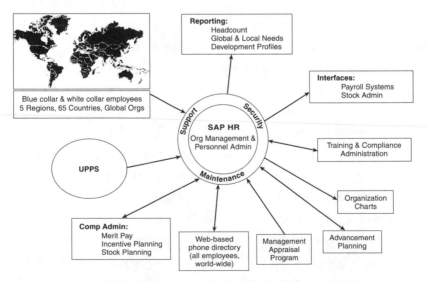

FIGURE 1-4 SAP HR: International Human Resources Technology.

Source: Mr. Mark Ready, Director, Human Resources Technology and Information, Kraft Foods Inc., October 19, 2005.

User IDs and passwords are required to log in to both systems, and both use employee ID numbers for user identification. On the SAP HR system, the employee ID is a randomly generated number. On UPPS, the employee ID is the employee's social security number. To better protect the employees' rights to privacy and to improve consistency between the UPPS and SAP HR systems, Kraft is in the process of changing its North American employee IDs from social security numbers to randomly generated numbers.[13]

All users are prohibited from allowing unauthorized individuals to use their login credentials, and they are warned to keep all passwords private. Forced password changes occur every forty-five days. If a user's account has not been accessed in sixty days, it is locked. Individuals who leave Kraft's employment have their accounts disabled on the day of their departure.[16]

Access to, and use of, the UPPS and SAP HR systems are restricted to those portions of the systems that are directly related to the employee's job responsibilities.[20] An Access Request Form must be completed by each individual requesting access to UPPS or SAP HR. The form requires the employee's name, identification number, title, function, and organizational dimension (i.e., Global Marketing, KNAC, KIC, Global Corporate Affairs, Global Finance, Global Human Resources, Global Information Systems, Global Law, Global Strategy and Business Development, Global Supply Chain, or Global Technology and Quality). The form must be signed by the employee, the employee's manager, the HR manager, and the Security Administrator at Kraft Foods Inc. If the employee requests access to data outside of his or her organizational dimension, a Security Access Exception Form also must be completed, in which the business reason for the additional access must be explained. This form must be signed by the employee, the employee's manager, the HR manager, the requisite Vice Presidents of all affected organizational dimensions, and the Security Administrator.[16]

Employees who are promoted, transferred to other organizational units, or otherwise change jobs within the organization have their access privileges adjusted to match their current job responsibilities. In addition, quarterly reports are generated by the systems so that all managers can verify the access rights of their employees.[16]

Each user who has access rights to employee data must sign a Human Resources Data Privacy Form, in which the user agrees to comply with Kraft's data privacy principles. The principles state that HR data must be accessed only by authorized users with a legitimate business need for that data. Access is restricted to those users who need to know the data to perform their jobs. In addition, users are granted the least privilege necessary to perform authorized tasks. All access to HR data is restricted to the fewest number of data fields possible, for the shortest time necessary, to carry out the job responsibilities.[21]

The data privacy principles also identify specific HR data that are considered sensitive, including social security number, home address, home telephone number, age/birth date, salary grade/pay information, job performance ratings, race or ethnic origin, religion, gender or sexual orientation, criminal records or charges, benefit choices (e.g., company-sponsored savings plans), political opinions, trade union membership, physical or mental health data, photographic images, participation in not-for-profit workplace-giving charities (e.g., United Way or Kraft Employee Fund), and all other personal data that could be used to identify a particular employee.[21]

Employee awareness of the importance of data security and ethical conduct is emphasized in the company's Code of Conduct. In 2003, the company issued a revised "Kraft Foods Code of Conduct for Compliance and Integrity"[22] describing Kraft's standards and expectations for acceptable employee behavior, particularly as it pertains to the work environment, company business practices, and the protection of company data. The Code of Conduct was made available online to employees and all managers were given a printed copy. In 2004, the "Code Overview" was released. It summarized those portions of the full-length Code of Conduct that were relevant to all employees. The "Code Overview" is available in twenty-nine languages. It has been made accessible to all employees in Kraft's global workforce, and a printed copy has been distributed to every employee below the level of manager.[23]

Kraft uses web-based training to help its employees understand the Code of Conduct policies and to reinforce the company's commitment to integrity. The interactive training courses use a series of realistic scenarios that are relevant to all business functions. The courses are developed by Integrity Interactive[24] using content established by Kraft Foods Inc. Since 2003, managers have been required to complete an annual online training course to demonstrate that they understand the key points of the Code of Conduct and to acknowledge that they will abide by the requirements of the code. Beginning in 2004, Kraft implemented additional web-based training courses for other employee groups to reinforce the importance of data privacy, ethical conduct, and acceptable behavior.

Final Comments

In November 2004, the Chairman and Chief Executive Officer of Altria Group, Inc., announced that Altria was beginning to prepare for a potential breakup of the company.[25] Since then, there has been growing speculation that Altria may spin off Kraft Foods Inc., allowing Kraft to become an independent company once again. It is possible that the spin off could occur in 2006, although Altria's decision will not be made until settlements have been reached in the multibillion dollar tobacco-related lawsuits that have been filed against Philip Morris.

In the meantime, ownership of the SAP HR system was transferred from Altria to Kraft in November 2005. There are plans to move all North American HR transactions from UPPS to SAP HR, and to make SAP HR the system of record for Kraft worldwide.[8]

Endnotes

1. U.S. Securities and Exchange Commission, Form 10-K, "Annual Report for the Year Ended December 31, 2004, Kraft Foods Inc." Available: http://www.sec.gov/Archives/edgar/data/1103982/000104746905006214/a2152234z10-K.htm.
2. "Kraft Brands." Available: http://www.kraft.com/brands/.
3. "Kraft Timeline." Available: http://www.kraft.com/100/timeline/index.html.
4. "Kraft Profile, Company Structure." Available: http://www.kraft.com/profile/company_structure.html.
5. "Kraft Profile, Management Team, Mark H. Berlind, Executive Vice President, Global Corporate Affairs." Available: http://kraft.com/profile/biosberlind.html.
6. "Kraft Profile, Management Team, James P. Dollive, Executive Vice President and Chief Financial Officer." Available: http://kraft.com/profile/biosdollive.html.
7. "Kraft Profile, Management Team, Terry M. Faulk, Executive Vice President, Global Human Resources." Available: http://kraft.com/profile/biosfaulk.html.
8. Personal communication with Mr. Mark Ready, Director, Human Resources Technology and Information, Kraft Foods Inc., August 1, 2005.
9. "Kraft Profile, Management Team, Marc Firestone, Executive Vice President, General Counsel and Corporate Secretary." Available: http://kraft.com/profile/biosfirestone.html.
10. "Kraft Profile, Management Team, Linda Hefner, Executive Vice President, Global Strategy and Business Development." Available: http://kraft.com/profile/bioshefner.html.
11. "Kraft Profile, Management Team, Franz-Josef Vogelsang, Executive Vice President, Global Supply Chain." Available: http://kraft.com/profile/biosvogelsang.html.

12. "Kraft Profile, Management Team, Jean Spence, Executive Vice President, Global Technology and Quality." Available: http://kraft.com/profile/biosspence.html.

13. Personal communication with Mr. Mark Ready, Director, Human Resources Technology and Information, Kraft Foods Inc., June 22, 2005.

14. "Directive 95/46/EC of the European Parliament and of the Council of 24 October 1995 on the protection of individuals with regard to the processing of personal data and on the free movement of such data." Available: http://europa.eu.int/eur-lex/lex/LexUriServ/LexUriServ.do?uri=CELEX:31995L0046:EN:HTML.

15. SAP is the largest software company in Europe and the fourth largest software company in the world. Headquartered in Walldorf, Germany, SAP was founded in 1972 as Systemanalyse und Programmentwicklung ("Systems, Applications and Products in Data Processing").

16. Personal communication with Mr. Mark Ready, Director, Human Resources Technology and Information, and Mr. Mike Kelly, Associate Director, Human Resources Technology and Information, Kraft Foods Inc., July 26, 2005.

17. Data Transfer Agreement between each of the Kraft entities in the EU member states and Kraft Foods International, Inc., 2002. Documentation provided by Mr. Mark Ready, Director, Human Resources Technology and Information, Kraft Foods Inc., August 1, 2005.

18. Personal communication with Ms. Debra Byars, Director, Global Information Risk Management, Kraft Foods Inc., July 26, 2005.

19. Citicus One software is a product of Citicus, Ltd. Available: http://www.citicus.com/index.asp.

20. Altria Group, Inc., "Electronic Information and Communications Policy, Version 3.0," February 1, 2005.

21. Kraft Foods Inc., "HR Data Privacy Principles." Personal communication with Mr. Mark Ready, Director, Human Resources

Technology and Information, and Mr. Mike Kelly, Associate Director, Human Resources Technology and Information, Kraft Foods Inc., July 26, 2005.

22. Kraft Foods Inc., "Kraft Foods Code of Conduct for Compliance and Integrity," April 2003. Available: http://www.kraft.com/pdfs/KraftFoods_CodeofConduct.pdf.

23. "Kraft Responsibility, Governance/Compliance and Integrity." Available: http://www.kraft.com/responsibility/governance_code_conduct.aspx.

24. "Integrity Interactive." Available: http://www.integrity-interactive.com/.

25. John Schmeltzer, "Altria preparing for breakup; Kraft independence lends hope for stock value boost." *Chicago Tribune*, November 5, 2004. Available: http://pqasb.pqarchiver.com/chicagotribune/.

CASE STUDY QUESTIONS

1. How does the EU Directive on the Protection of Personal Data impose requirements on organizations in non-EU countries?
2. How does Kraft comply with EU data privacy regulations governing the protection of employee data?
3. The EU directive requires "appropriate technical and organizational controls" to be in place to protect the confidentiality and integrity of personal data. How can an organization determine whether its security controls are appropriate?
4. What user access controls are in place for the UPPS and SAP HR systems?
5. How does Kraft implement the following access controls: need to know; least privilege; mandatory access control; and role-based access control?
6. Identify at least ten examples of specific HR data that are considered sensitive at Kraft Foods Inc.

7. What is the purpose of Kraft's Code of Conduct for Compliance and Integrity? How is this information distributed to Kraft employees?

8. Why is Kraft moving away from the use of employee social security numbers for user identification on UPPS?

9. Through the UPPS, Kraft provides its employees online access to their own employee data. Why would Kraft do this?

10. Why would Kraft want to move all of its North American HR transactions from UPPS to SAP HR?

KEY TERMS

British Standard 7799 (BS 7799): Code of practice for establishing an information security management system. It was first published by the National Standards Body of the United Kingdom in 1995. It establishes guidelines for information security controls; it consists of two parts. Part I provides a detailed and comprehensive list of good security practices. Part II summarizes the security controls and provides specifications for an information security management system. In 2000, Part I was published as International Organization for Standardization/International Electrotechnical Commission (ISO/IEC) 17799.

Business Continuity Planning: Methodology for developing a strategy to minimize the effect of a disruptive event and to allow for the resumption of critical business processes.

Disaster Recovery Planning: Methodology for developing a comprehensive statement of actions for responding to an emergency.

Human Resources Technology and Information (HRT&I): Specialized group within the Global Human Resources function that works closely with Global Information Systems on human resources–related technology projects.

International Organization for Standardization/International Electrotechnical Commission 17799 (ISO/IEC 17799): See BS 7799.

KIC: Kraft International Commercial.

KNAC: Kraft North America Commercial.

Risk Assessment: Process of analyzing the threats to, and vulnerabilities of, a system, and evaluating the possible impact and probability of occurrence associated with each potential loss event.

Risk Management: Process of identifying and assessing risk, and evaluating and selecting alternative responses to risk, based on the consideration of legal, economic, political, and social factors.

Risk Remediation: Process of taking action to reduce risk exposure.

SAP HR: Enterprise resource planning system from SAP. System used for human resources transaction processing for all international employees at Kraft Foods Inc.

Sarbanes-Oxley Act of 2002: U.S. law created to protect investors by improving the reliability and accuracy of corporate disclosures. It establishes stringent financial reporting requirements for publicly traded companies. The law is named after its sponsors: Senator Paul Sarbanes (D–MD) and Representative Michael Oxley (R–OH). See http://news.findlaw.com/hdocs/docs/gwbush/sarbanesoxley072302.pdf.

Shared Service Center (SSC): Provides online accessibility to human resources transactions for North American employees of Kraft Foods Inc.

Threat Analysis: Systematic examination of circumstances that have the potential to cause loss or harm.

Unified Personnel and Payroll System (UPPS): System used for human resources transaction processing for all North American employees of Kraft Foods Inc.

Vulnerability Analysis: Systematic examination to identify exploitable weaknesses in a system, in the use of the system, its procedures, and its internal controls.

ADVO, INC.:

INTEGRATING IT AND PHYSICAL SECURITY

C omplacency is often the greatest threat to security. It is easy to overlook or underestimate potential security threats until they become a reality, and it is equally easy to lose focus on those security threats once the immediate crisis has passed. Advo, Inc., successfully overcame these challenges.

This case study describes how two national crises triggered immediate changes in Advo's physical security and process security controls. It also describes Advo's treatment of information technology (IT) and physical security as interconnected components of the organization's evolving security infrastructure. To provide necessary background information, the case study begins with an overview of Advo, Inc., its operations, and the security controls that were in place before the occurrence of the 9/11 terrorist attacks and the subsequent anthrax attacks.

Advo, Inc.—The Company

Advo, Inc. is the largest provider of direct mail advertising services in the United States. Advo processes and distributes printed advertising from its 25,000 clients to more than 112 million consumer households throughout the United States and Canada. Its clients are the manufacturers, retailers, and service companies whose products and services are used by the general public. They include supermarkets, drug stores, quick serve restaurants, home furnishing retailers, and discount and department stores.[1]

Advo's 2004 reported net income was $48.7 million on total revenue of $1.2 billion. Headquartered in Windsor, Connecticut, Advo currently has twenty-one mail processing facilities located throughout the United States. The company employs approximately 3,900 full- and part-time employees. It also hires outside temporary employees for certain production jobs and for assistance during busy seasons.[1]

Founded as a delivery company in 1929, Advo entered the direct mail industry as a solo mailer in 1946. Advo's shared mail program began in 1980, when it combined advertisements from different businesses and distributed them together.[1]

In 1985, Advo partnered with the National Center for Missing and Exploited Children and the United States Postal Service (USPS) to establish the America's Looking For Its Missing Children program. It is the most successful private-sector program of its kind. Its Have You Seen Me? cards, which show the names and faces of missing children, are viewed by more than 120 million people each week and have become the nation's most recognized piece of mail.[2]

Within the past decade, Advo has expanded its size through company acquisitions. One of its most significant acquisitions occurred in February 1998, when it purchased The Mailhouse, Inc., a franchise-based cooperative coupon mail company. It was renamed MailCoups, Inc., shortly after its acquisition. Headquartered in Taunton, Massachusetts, MailCoups, Inc., operates as a wholly owned subsidiary of Advo. Franchise licenses are sold under the brand name SuperCoups. The franchises create coupons for local merchants and mail the coupons in a distinctive-looking envelope (http://www.supercoups.com). By the end of September 2004, there were 225 franchise units in twenty-three states.[1]

In November 2000, Advo acquired Mail Marketing Systems, Inc., a direct mail advertising company located in Maryland. It operates as a wholly owned subsidiary of Advo, and it provides mail coverage to approximately 4.5 million households.[1] Advo acquired the New Jersey Shoppers Guide in April 2001. The direct mail shopping guide has a weekly circulation of approximately 400,000 households in Southern New Jersey.[1] Advo's most recent acquisition occurred in June 2002, when it purchased FACC Corporation, a direct mail advertising firm based in Canada. Shortly after its acquisition, FACC Corporation was renamed Advo Canada. In 2004, Advo Canada was renamed First Avenue. The company, which operates as a wholly owned subsidiary of Advo, mails approximately 220 million pieces of advertising each year to targeted segments of Canada's twelve million households.[1]

Advo also has formed several newspaper alliances, which it uses to further expand the distribution of its clients' advertising material. Its alliances with Gannett Company, Inc., MediaNews Group, Inc., Knight-Ridder, Inc., Freedom Communications, The New York Times Company, St. Petersburg Times, E.W. Scripps Company, and The Tribune Company[1] enable Advo's advertising material to be distributed to the newspapers' subscribers.

Operations

Advo, Inc., is the largest commercial user of USPS standard mail. The printed advertising from its 25,000 clients is distributed to more than 112 million consumer households through the company's solo and shared mail services.[1]

Advo's solo mail service consists of addressing and processing individual client brochures and circulars for distribution through the USPS. The pieces can be processed using the mailing lists provided by Advo or the client. Solo mail service tends to be chosen by two types of clients: those who want to maintain a separate image and total control over when and to whom their advertisements are mailed, or those who want their advertisements sent to areas where Advo's shared mail service does not exist.[1]

Advo's shared mail service is brand named ShopWise. A four-page, colored magazine surrounds a mail package, which consists of advertisements from businesses located in a specific mailing area. Larger businesses usually provide Advo with printed advertising materials in preset quantities, whereas smaller retail clients rely on Advo to perform graphics services or to act as a broker for printing operations. The mail packages are addressed using Advo's mailing list, and the company sorts and transports the mailings for USPS delivery.[1] In April 2000, Advo established a companion, opt-in website named ShopWise.com (http://www.shopwise.com). The site enables retailers to supplement their mailed advertisements by providing consumers with online coupons and special e-mail offers.[1]

Most of Advo's revenue is derived from its ShopWise program, which is believed to be the largest advertising program of its kind. Shared mail advertisements are delivered each week to approximately seventy-eight million consumer households in more than 130 different markets. An additional thirty-four million households are reached through the Advo National Network Extension program.[1] This program allows Advo to provide its clients with a wider advertising distribution through the network's membership of regional shared mail companies.

Advo's mailing list is used by the company to target mailings to specific consumers. Advo also rents portions of its mailing list to other direct marketing organizations. Believed to be the largest residential mailing list in the nation, it contains the addresses of almost all of the households in the United States. In addition to its more than 130 million household addresses, it includes more than 12.6 million business addresses, all arranged in mail delivery sequence order.[1]

The printed advertising materials from Advo's clients are processed by approximately 1,700 production employees who work at twenty-one mail processing facilities throughout the United States. The locations of these facilities are shown in Table 2-1. At each of the company's facilities, inserting machines are used to collate the individual advertising pieces into packages, and addressing and labeling equipment is used to process the materials for mailing. The mailings are sorted by the company's transportation department, verified by the USPS at an on-site Detached Mail Unit located at each facility, and transported to a local post office for timely delivery by individual postal carriers.[1]

Security Controls Before the Terrorist and Bioterrorist-Related Attacks

Until September 2001, Advo's security controls were indiscriminate and noncohesive.[3] No formal security policies or procedures had been established, and everyone viewed security as a low priority. At corporate

---

TABLE 2-1 Locations of Advo's Mail Processing Facilities*

Atlanta, Georgia	Orlando, Florida
Cincinnati, Ohio	Philadelphia, Pennsylvania
Dallas, Texas	Pittsburgh, Pennsylvania
Denver, Colorado	Phoenix, Arizona
Detroit, Michigan	Salt Lake City, Utah
Houston, Texas	San Francisco, California
Los Angeles (1), California	Seattle, Washington
Los Angeles (2), California	Taunton, Massachusetts
Memphis, Tennessee	Washington, D.C.
Miami, Florida	Windsor, Connecticut
Milwaukee, Wisconsin	

*Advo owns the Windsor, Connecticut facility. The remaining twenty facilities are leased.

Source: Frank LaMorte, Director of Corporate Security, Advo, Inc., March 31, 2005.

headquarters, the controls primarily consisted of security guard services and employee background checks. Both were provided by outside agencies. Burns International Services Corporation (known today as Securitas Security Services USA, Inc.) had been hired to provide security guard services. Guards were present at night, but minimal security existed during business hours. A temporary agency had been hired to perform a pre-employment background check on all employees. It consisted of little more than a basic civil background check.[3]

Security was weaker at the company's mail processing facilities. Employee background checks were superficial, if they were performed at all. Seventy percent of the facilities' workers were temporary employees whose backgrounds were not checked before they were hired. A contract-level guard service provided uniform visibility, but little else. Most of the facilities were located in industrial areas where urban crime problems were commonplace. These facilities often had poor outdoor lighting, inadequate fencing, and no security cameras. Employees were at risk of attack as they walked across the parking lots, the facilities were not protected from the risk of car bombs, and there was little control over who was in a facility at any given time. Emergency exit doors were frequently propped open. Visitors were not monitored, and contractors were allowed to freely wander around the facilities.[3]

Neither corporate headquarters nor any of the facilities had mailrooms to handle incoming mail. Packages and other types of mail were left inside the building, near the front entrance.[3] There were other security vulnerabilities common to all locations. Sensitive documents were discarded in their entirety. Keys to interior offices and exterior doors were not carefully controlled or managed. Plans for business continuity and disaster recovery were inconclusive and undocumented.[3]

Although physical security was weak, considerably stronger controls were in place to protect Advo's critical applications and databases. In July 1996, Advo entered into a ten-year agreement with IBM Global Services[4] to provide computer processing, systems development and systems legacy support to Advo. Advo's proprietary databases and enterprise applications were stored and processed on more than two dozen servers in IBM's Southbury, Connecticut, facility. Included were data pertaining to Advo's order processing and production control systems, transportation and distribution systems, billing and financial systems, human resources and payroll processing systems, address list maintenance files, label printing and distribution systems, carrier routing of addresses from client files, and market and demographic analyses.[1] Long-term agreements were signed with IBM to provide server farm management services and to provide security services for Advo's applications and data. IBM's security services included provisions for real-time system monitoring, intrusion detection and prevention, and incident management.

Terrorist and Bioterrorist-Related Attacks

Many of Advo's executive officers were in New York City on the morning of September 11, 2001.[3] The CEO and several senior-level managers from the company's Operating Committee were in Manhattan when American Airlines Flight 11 and United Airlines Flight 175 hit the North and South Towers of the World Trade Center.

The terrorist attacks elevated the importance of security within Advo. There was an abrupt and dramatic change in executive attitudes and physical security was given top priority. Advo's CEO, in consultation with the Senior Vice President of Fulfillment, mandated that a real security presence be established at all locations. The Wackenhut Corporation was immediately hired to provide uniformed security officers on a 24–7 basis at Advo's corporate headquarters and at all mail processing facilities.[3]

The crisis was far from over. Less than two weeks after the 9/11 attacks, the first bioterrorism-related anthrax attack occurred.[5] Public fears grew as media reports of anthrax-laced mail increased. By the end of the first week of October, the first anthrax-related death had been reported. The origin of the anthrax was tied to a letter that the victim had handled. By mid-October, two postal workers had died from anthrax exposure. Public fears escalated into widespread panic. Media coverage was continuous and heightened by reports that several high-profile individuals had been targeted to receive anthrax-contaminated letters, including former NBC News anchor Tom Brokaw, Senator Tom Daschle (D–SD), and Senator Patrick Leahy (D–VT). By December 5, a total of twenty-two cases of anthrax had been identified: eleven were confirmed as inhalation anthrax[6] and eleven were cutaneous anthrax.[6] Most of the cases involved individuals who worked at postal facilities in New Jersey and the District of Columbia, where anthrax-contaminated letters were handled or processed. Other cases involved individuals who worked at media companies in New York City or Florida, where letters contaminated with anthrax were handled.[7]

The impact of the anthrax attacks was dramatic. To the general public, nothing seemed to be safe anymore, not even the mail. Citizens became suspicious of the envelopes and packages delivered to them, and those most gripped in panic refused to open their mail at all.

The USPS faced a crisis of confidence from the general population and from its employees. The results of environmental anthrax testing caused the USPS to temporarily close several postal facilities in the Washington, D.C., and Trenton, New Jersey, areas. To allay public fears, the USPS sent a direct mail postcard to every household and post office box in the United States, and to all military Army Post Office and Fleet Post Office addresses.[8] The postcard contained information for handling suspicious or contaminated letters and packages.[8]

For a company like Advo, whose business relies on the USPS and whose clients rely on people opening their mail, the anthrax attacks posed a significant threat to its existence.

Advo's Response to the Anthrax Attacks

By early October, many of Advo's 25,000 clients had expressed concern over the safety of their mailings. They worried that if their advertisements became contaminated with anthrax, they could be put out of business. Advo's top management was concerned that cross-contamination could occur in the company's mail processing facilities. The USPS provided some of the equipment Advo used to process its clients' printed advertising materials. If the equipment were contaminated with anthrax, the spores could be transferred to Advo's mailings.

Advo's CEO, in consultation with the Senior Vice President of Fulfillment, mandated that all of the company's mail processing equipment be cleaned regularly. A cleaning process was established, which called for the use of hand wands to spray a chlorine-based solution on equipment that was hanging up on a conveyor. The process, which had been approved by the U.S. Environmental Protection Agency, turned out to be cumbersome, foul-smelling, and potentially risky because it was performed inside of the mail processing facilities.[3] A better process was implemented in which the equipment, upon delivery by the USPS, was cleaned in an adjacent trailer before it was moved inside a mail processing facility.[3]

Strengthening Security

On October 26, 2001, the company's Senior Vice President of Fulfillment was made the Senior Vice President of Security Management.[9] The change in title was significant; it represented the company's commitment to security and it signaled a change in the company's approach. Enterprise-wide security improvements would be made, and the individual in charge of orchestrating those improvements was a member of senior management.

Because there was little in-house expertise to provide necessary guidance, consultants were hired. Kroll, Inc., was hired to do a risk analysis of the company's physical security, and Ernst & Young was hired to do a risk analysis of IT security.[3] Their recommendations included the hiring of additional employees in IT and physical security.

In March 2002, Advo hired a Director of IT Security and Enterprise Architecture. The following month, Advo hired a Director of Corporate Security. Both were positions of authority. The Director of IT Security and Enterprise Architecture reported directly to the Chief Information Officer (CIO) and indirectly to the Senior Vice President of Security Management. The Director of Corporate Security reported to the Senior Vice President of Security Management. Both the CIO and the Senior Vice President of Security Management reported to the CEO.[3]

The Senior Vice President of Security Management convened weekly meetings with both directors to discuss physical and IT security. Collaboration and cooperation were viewed as essential, and both directors were empowered to find solutions to the company's security challenges.[3]

The Director of IT Security and Enterprise Architecture was allowed to hire consultants when needed to address Advo's most critical IT concerns. These concerns included improving the data center at corporate headquarters, implementing stronger software countermeasures, physically protecting its computer systems, establishing tighter access controls for enterprise applications, monitoring network usage, and developing the company's disaster recovery plan.[3]

The use of IT consultants was consistent with Advo's business model. Almost twelve terabytes of data were stored on thirty-two Regatta servers at IBM's Southbury, Connecticut, site.[10] IBM Global Services[4] was responsible for protecting that data. Each year, it issued a GSD331 document, which detailed IBM's guidelines for best practices in information security. The GSD331 provisions broadly map to British Standard (BS) 7799, and they include Information Security Policy, Security Organization, Asset Classification and Control, Personnel Security, Physical and Environmental Security, Computer and Network Management, System Access Control, Systems Development and Maintenance, Business Continuity Planning, and Compliance.[11] PricewaterhouseCoopers was hired to evaluate the security controls identified in GSD331, and it issued its opinion in a Statement on Auditing Standards (SAS) 70 report.[12]

The Director of IT Security and Enterprise Architecture was responsible for determining employee access rights to all data and applications. These permissions were established through the use of role-based access control.[10] The Director of Corporate Security was responsible for ensuring that all necessary physical security measures were implemented and enforced at corporate headquarters and all facilities. These security measures included perimeter protection, physical access controls, and response procedures. By September 2002, 109 new employees had been hired in physical security.[3] Most of the personnel increases occurred at the mail processing facilities, where significant improvements had been made.

Each facility had a lead security officer who was assisted by three security associates. A tour management system from Tiscor (a mobile software solutions provider)[13] was implemented at all locations. The system required each security associate to use a Palm Pilot to scan preestablished inspection points located throughout the building. For example, coded entries near exit doors and fire extinguishers were used to ensure that the security associates conducted their security tours.[3]

Improved outdoor lighting and perimeter fencing were installed. Inside, the facilities were divided into sections that could be separately controlled. Non-employees were restricted from openly wandering around the facilities. Visitors were required to meet with their employee contacts at a front reception area. Each visitor was required to wear a visitor badge and to sign a log book upon arrival and departure.[3] Packages and other types of mail were delivered to mailrooms, which had been established at all locations.[3]

At corporate headquarters, the Senior Vice President of Security Management had a Vice President and two Directors of Corporate Security reporting directly to him. The two directors had nine security managers between them. Every six months, each Security Manager visited two or three mail processing facilities, ensuring that all of the facilities were visited twice a year.[3]

By September 28, 2002, Advo had spent $5.7 million on increased security: $2.4 million had been spent on operational security costs, and

$3.3 million had been spent on Selling, General, and Administrative security costs.[14]

By the end of 2003, many security policies and procedures had been formulated (Table 2-2). However, many more still awaited top management's approval. An administrative bottleneck had formed at corporate headquarters, inadvertently created by the increasing number of senior-level managers who reported to the Senior Vice President of Security.[15] Efficiency needed to be improved and costs needed to be contained. An integrated security management system provided the solution.

Integrated Security Management System

In 2004, Advo implemented a security management system[16] that enables all of the company's facilities to be connected to a Security Control Center (SCC) at corporate headquarters. Access to the SCC is restricted to authorized employees who must enter and exit through a mantrap. The SCC operates twenty-four hours a day, seven days a week, and it requires a staff of no more than two employees at any time. Those employees must have already passed a detailed background check, including a criminal background check, prior employment verification, and drug screening.[10]

The security management system integrates the company's security applications, including employee identification badges, visitor controls, parking permits, security tour controls, alarm systems, security cameras, and support measures for incident investigations. It also allows the SCC to exercise centralized control of these applications at all locations.

Employee identification badges are created in the SCC. Each badge includes an employee photograph. The badges are programmed for access control purposes and the data are stored in the security management system database. Badge access is required to enter any facility, and to enter specific areas within a facility. There is real-time access control. Using the security management system software, the SCC can observe all entries,

TABLE 2-2 Some of Advo's Security Policies and Procedures

TOPIC	POLICY/PROCEDURE
Access control	Access Control Policy
Bomb threats	Bomb Threat Response Policy
	Bomb Threat Response Procedure
	Emergency Action Plan—Bomb Threat Response
Cleaning USPS equipment	Cleaning Outbound Equipment Procedure
Dark hours	Dark Hours Procedure
Emergency action plan	Emergency Action Plan
Fencing/utility security	Fencing Policy
	Securing Building Utilities Policy
Key control	Facility Key Control Policy
	Key Control Procedure
Laptop security	Laptop Computer Security Policy
	How Do I Secure Computer Equipment?
Lighting	Lighting Policy
Locking devices	Locking Devices Policy
Mailroom security	Mailroom Policy
	Mailroom Procedure
Parking control	Parking Control Policy
	Parking Control Procedure
Pre-employment screening	Pre-Employment Screening Policy
	Pre-Employment Drug Testing Policy
Records	Record Retention Policy
Security badges	Security Identification Badge Procedure
Security cameras	Use of Security Cameras Policy
Security incident reporting	Security Incident Reporting Policy
	Security Incident Reporting Procedure
Security associates	Security Officer Policy
	Security Officer Tour Management System Policy
	Security Officer Procedure

(continues)

TABLE 2-2 Some of Advo's Security Policies and Procedures *(continued)*

TOPIC	POLICY/PROCEDURE
Transportation security	Transportation Security—Use of Seals Procedure
	Transportation ID Database Procedure
Unidentified material	Emergency Action Plan—Suspicious Material
	Credible Threat Evaluation Guidelines
	Fact Finding Questionnaire
Utility failure	Utility Failure—Electric—Procedure
	Utility Failure—Electric—Assessment Guide
	Utility Failure—Electric—Analysis/Action Guide
Workplace violence	Workplace Violence Prevention Policy

Source: Personal communication with Frank LaMorte, Director of Corporate Security, Advo, Inc., March 31, 2005.

monitor rejected accesses, and modify access privileges. For example, it can allow an employee who is visiting another facility to gain temporary access, or it can disallow a former employee from entering the premises.[10]

Visitor controls are imposed through an extended application of the security management system. Employees can pre-register their visitors through the company's intranet, which reduces the number of unexpected visitors. Visitor badges can be printed in advance, resulting in shorter visitor waiting times and fewer visitors in the reception area.

Parking permits are issued to all employees by an on-site security technician. Employee vehicle information is stored in the security management system database. Visitor vehicle information is recorded in the Visitor and Vehicle Log. Parking is restricted to designated areas, and the employee, visitor, and shipping/receiving lots are clearly marked.

The electronic gates at the employee and shipping/receiving lots can be controlled by the transportation department at each facility, or by the SCC through the security management system.

A minimum of two interior and two exterior security tours are conducted every day at all facilities. The security tours are performed by on-site security technicians using a tour management system from Tiscor.[13] This system interfaces with the security management system.

All of the alarm systems (e.g., panic alarms, fire alarms) at every facility can be monitored by the SCC through the security management system. Security cameras are situated in the vicinity of the alarm systems, as well as at other key locations inside and outside of each facility. The cameras produce color images that can be viewed in real time on multiple monitors in the SCC. All cameras are equipped with digital video recording capabilities for security investigation and identification purposes.[10]

System Security

The security management system software is stored on a hardened Windows 2003 server in the data center located at corporate headquarters.[3] Access to the data center is restricted to authorized employees, and an employee identification badge is needed to gain entry. Also in the data center are between thirty and forty servers that provide essential capabilities, such as Internet connectivity, e-mail communication, and non-critical applications to corporate headquarters and to all of Advo's facilities. User authentication is established by means of password entry during login. User passwords must be at least five characters long and they must be changed at least once every ninety days.[10]

In addition to the servers in the data center, there are two servers at each facility for e-mail and office automation. There also are kiosk PCs located on the shop floor of every facility. The kiosk PCs are connected to the company's intranet and can be used to access the Internet. Currently, no login is required for these systems, which can be used by more than 125 temporary employees who work on the shop floor of each mail processing facility. This practice is expected to change by 2006, when a password login procedure will be enforced.[10]

To keep all software patches current, the Director of IT Security and Enterprise Architecture uses Novell ZENworks Patch Management, an automated system that sends executable files to patch systems across the enterprise. To protect against virus infections, antivirus software from Symantec Corporation is automatically updated every hour and the updates are immediately distributed to all systems.[10]

Several tools are used to monitor and protect Advo's computer networks. Websense Enterprise Explorer 5.2 is used to filter Internet data, track employee Internet usage, block unwanted sites, and provide data about systems infected with spyware. Mazu Profiler, an intrusion prevention system from Mazu Networks, Inc., is used to monitor and audit the use of Advo's networks. In addition, six Snort sensors help to provide network intrusion detection system capabilities. One of the sensors is located at IBM Global Services in Southbury, Connecticut, where Advo's critical applications and databases are stored. Five other Snort sensors are located at corporate headquarters: at the data center, at the virtual private network, at the demilitarized zone, inside the firewall, and outside the firewall.[10]

Both the data center and the SCC have an on-site uninterruptible power supply provided by a diesel generator with a 250-gallon diesel tank. A backup site for the data center and the SCC was completed in September 2005. Located about four miles away from corporate headquarters in Windsor, Connecticut, the site provides complete system redundancy; it operates on its own power grid with separate backup power.[10]

Advo purchased the Living Disaster Recovery Planning System from Strohl Systems Group, Inc.,[17] to ensure continued operations in the event of a catastrophe. Disaster recovery plans were developed for corporate headquarters, including the data center and the SCC. A disaster recovery plan also was developed for the Philadelphia, Pennsylvania, mail processing facility. This plan will be used as a model for disaster recovery at all of the company's mail processing facilities.

Security Audits

In December 2004, Advo's security managers conducted a security audit at corporate headquarters in Windsor, Connecticut, and at each of the twenty-one mail processing facilities. The audit was designed to evaluate the controls implemented through the integrated security management system. The audit covered twenty-one key areas: access controls, bomb threats, cleaning of equipment, dark hours,[18] emergency action plan, fencing, identification badges, key control, laptop security, lighting, locking devices, mailroom, parking control, pre-employment screening, record access and retention, security cameras, security incident reporting, security officers and technicians, tour management system, utility security, and workplace violence.[10] Appendix A lists specific audit points for each of these key areas.

A weighted score was assigned to each audit point, using a rating system established by the security managers. The audit results were compiled in a one-page, color-coded report for top management. This report enabled top management to target specific security improvements at individual facilities.

Advo now conducts security audits semiannually. The audit areas and specific audit points are reviewed each year and revised when needed to reflect the industry's best practices. The company believes that frequent audits reinforce the importance of security and help to ingrain a security mindset throughout the organization.

Final Comments

Advo's successful transformation into a security-conscious company can be attributed to three factors. First, top management's attention remains focused on the need for stronger security, long after the Fall 2001 crises have passed. Second, the Director of IT Security and Enterprise Architecture and the Director of Corporate Security occupy positions of authority who report directly to top management. From this level, they are able to institute necessary changes. Third, IT and physical security are not treated as disparate entities, but as interconnected components of the organization's security infrastructure.

The integrated security management system has allowed Advo to achieve a greater level of security with fewer employees. By the end of 2004, thirty employees remained in physical security, down from 109. Also, a flatter organizational structure has been created. Top management has eliminated the positions of seven security managers and a vice president who reported to the Senior Vice President of Security.[15] Only two directors and two security managers remain.[10] Implementing the security management system has improved efficiency and lowered costs by $3.3 million.

Appendix A:
Key Areas and Specific Audit Points

TABLE 2-3 Access Controls

Were all perimeter entry points kept closed and locked or secured with locked scissor gates at all times?

Were truckers always restricted to the trucker's lounge?

According to SCC records, were emergency exits used only for emergencies during the last month?

Did all visitors and contractors register with the receptionist or other authorized person and receive a badge before entering the office or production areas?

Did a responsible employee screen incoming workers at the beginning of each shift when a security technician or officer was not available?

(continues)

TABLE 2-3 Access Controls *(continued)*

Was a list of expected temporary employees available for screening incoming workers at the beginning of each shift?

Were all visitors for the last four business days properly signed in and out of the visitor log?

Were all visitors (except trusted contractors) consistently escorted inside the office and production areas?

Were only authorized persons observed inside the facility?

Was the electronically controlled truck gate kept closed at all times except when a vehicle was entering or leaving?

Was the electronically controlled employee gate kept closed at all times except when a vehicle was entering or leaving?

Source: Personal communication with Frank LaMorte, Director of Corporate Security, Advo, Inc., March 31, 2005.

TABLE 2-4 Bomb Threats

Has the receptionist been trained to respond properly in the event of a bomb threat?

Is the Telephonic Bomb Threat Report readily available at the receptionist's workstation?

Is a documented volunteer search team in place?

Has the search team received documented bomb search training within the last twelve months?

Is the USPS Suspicious Mail poster posted in the mailroom?

Has a bomb threat muster point, at least 1,000 feet from the facility, been identified?

Has a letter bomb safety point been designated for minimizing risk from a suspicious package?

Source: Personal communication with Frank LaMorte, Director of Corporate Security, Advo, Inc., March 31, 2005.

TABLE 2-5 Cleaning of Equipment

Is a suitable backpack spray unit present, in good condition, and deployable if needed?

Is a full set of personal protection equipment (gloves, face shield, rain pants, rain coat) present, in good condition, and usable if needed?

Is a copy of the Cleaning of Equipment training program available on site?

Are suitable drying fans present, in good condition, and usable if needed?

Source: Personal communication with Frank LaMorte, Director of Corporate Security, Advo, Inc., March 31, 2005.

TABLE 2-6 Dark Hours

Do SCC records show that dark hours monitoring was properly requested and terminated during the last five periods when the building was unoccupied during the audit period?

Source: Personal communication with Frank LaMorte, Director of Corporate Security, Advo, Inc., March 31, 2005.

TABLE 2-7 Emergency Action Plan

Is the Facility Emergency Directory for this location up to date?

Is a documented Emergency Response Team in place?

Are evacuation routes clearly marked with standard signage, or on diagrams posted conspicuously throughout the building?

Are severe weather shelter areas clearly marked?

Are exterior evacuation muster points designated and posted?

Source: Personal communication with Frank LaMorte, Director of Corporate Security, Advo, Inc., March 31, 2005.

TABLE 2-8 Fencing

Are the shipping and loading dock areas of the facility protected with a perimeter fence?

Are the shipping and loading dock areas of the facility protected by an electrically operated gate?

Are the fence and gates at least eight feet high?

Is the distance between the bottom of the gate and the paved surface four inches or less?

Is the gate equipped with a siren-activated emergency release?

Is a fail safe device in place to prevent gate closure with a vehicle in the opening?

Does the fence have a horizontal bottom rail?

Does the fence have a horizontal top rail or tension wire?

Is there an adequate clear zone on both sides of the fence?

Are the fence and gate(s) fully intact (no visible damage)?

Is the required signage in place for siren-activated emergency access devices? Emergency exits? Access hours? Contact number for emergencies (SCC)?

Source: Personal communication with Frank LaMorte, Director of Corporate Security, Advo, Inc., March 31, 2005.

TABLE 2-9 Identification Badges

Were all employees in the facility wearing the issued security badge in a plainly visible manner at the time of the audit?

Were all vendors and temporary contractors working in the facility wearing the issued security badge in a plainly visible manner at the time of the audit?

Are temporary badges issued to temporary field staff at the beginning of each shift and collected and audited at the end of that shift?

(continues)

TABLE 2-9 Identification Badges *(continued)*

Are steady shipping contractors issued contractor identification badges?

Do badge audits show that temporary badges were consistently returned by the end of the day when they were issued on each of the last ten days?

Are temporary badge stocks audited each business day?

Are lost or missing badges immediately deactivated when discovered during audits?

Source: Personal communication with Frank LaMorte, Director of Corporate Security, Advo, Inc., March 31, 2005.

TABLE 2-10 Key Control

Are all non-issued keys stored in a securely locked cabinet?

Are non-issued keys clearly labeled and well organized?

Does the person responsible for key issuance (and up to one backup individual) have the only keys to the key cabinet?

Are accurate and properly signed key accountability forms on file for all keys issued to randomly selected employees who have been issued keys?

Is an up-to-date key tracking log maintained by the person responsible for key issuance?

Does an inspection of the key tracking log show that ten randomly selected key accountability forms are properly entered on the log?

Source: Personal communication with Frank LaMorte, Director of Corporate Security, Advo, Inc., March 31, 2005.

TABLE 2-11 Laptop Security

Were all unattended laptop computers observed during the audit secured to a fixed object with an Advo-approved locking device or portable alarm?

Source: Personal communication with Frank LaMorte, Director of Corporate Security, Advo, Inc., March 31, 2005.

TABLE 2-12 Lighting

Are adequate lighting levels maintained in the following exterior areas? Main entrance, employee entrance, receiving entrance, trucker's lounge entrance, employee parking lot, truck court, employee entrance gate, truck gate, sidewalks, building perimeter.

Are adequate lighting levels maintained in the following interior areas? Warehouse, administrative office, production floor, transportation office.

Source: Personal communication with Frank LaMorte, Director of Corporate Security, Advo, Inc., March 31, 2005.

TABLE 2-13 Locking Devices

Are all newly installed locking devices in conformity with the list of devices approved by the Vice President of Corporate Services?

Are the following interior doors secured with adequate and properly functioning locking devices? Reception door to office, all managers' offices, all doors between office and production floor or warehouse, server room, all storage rooms containing valuable or confidential materials, mail room.

Are all of the following exterior doors secured with adequate and properly functioning locking devices? Main entrance to reception, production employee entrance, receiving entrance.

Does the facility have a maximum of three exterior key cylinders (at the main entrance, employees' entrance, and receiving entrance)?

Are the three exterior cylinders equipped with removable cores?

Is a spare set of removable cores and keys available for immediate replacement of the exterior cylinders if necessary?

Are card reader-controlled locks in place at the following doors? Main entry vestibule to reception, employee entrance, receiving entrance, all production floor office doors, server room, mail room, door between break room and office, reception area door to office.

Are only Advo-issued locks used on employees' lockers?

Source: Personal communication with Frank LaMorte, Director of Corporate Security, Advo, Inc., March 31, 2005.

TABLE 2-14 Mailroom

Has a Mail Security Coordinator been appointed?

Has a Deputy Mail Security Coordinator been appointed?

Was the mailroom kept locked at all times during the audit?

Is the mailroom door equipped with a card reader?

If the mailroom door is not equipped with a card reader, is a Mail Room Entry Log sign in/sign out procedure in place and adhered to?

Are the Mail Room Entry Logs kept on file for a minimum of one year?

Is access to the mailroom effectively restricted to the Mail Room Security Coordinator and Deputy?

Are all small USPS, FEDEX, UPS, and courier deliveries made directly to the mailroom?

Do the Mail Security Coordinator and Deputy Coordinator keep the screening criteria in the current USPS Mail Center Security Guide readily available in the mailroom?

Are all materials delivered to the mailroom consistently screened in accordance with the USPS Mail Center Security Guide before being stored or placed in mailboxes?

Are Parcel Delivery Notices being consistently used to notify employees of packages too large to fit in the assigned mailbox?

Are securely locked mailboxes in consistent daily use?

Source: Personal communication with Frank LaMorte, Director of Corporate Security, Advo, Inc., March 31, 2005.

TABLE 2-15 Parking Control

Is an effective parking permit control system in effect at this facility?

Is conspicuous signage in place to give notice that parking is restricted to authorized vehicles only?

Is conspicuous signage in place to give notice that unauthorized vehicles are subject to tow?

Is conspicuous signage in place to designate spaces reserved for visitors?

(continues)

TABLE 2-15 Parking Control *(continued)*

Is an agreement with a towing vendor currently in place?

Are private vehicles effectively restricted from parking in any portion of the shipping/receiving lot?

Are trailers parked only at shipping/receiving doors or on a trailer pad in the lot?

Are all of the vehicles in the parking area at the time of the audit in compliance with either the requirement to display a valid parking permit or the requirement to register the vehicle in the visitor log?

Are all parking permits affixed to the vehicles in conformity with the display requirements of the Parking Control Procedure?

Does the temporary staffing agency at the facility provide a current list of all of that agency's assigned employees with their vehicle information to the facility as required?

Is the Parking Permit Log maintained, current, and complete?

Is the Parking Permit Log from the previous year still on file and available for inspection?

Are all vehicles parked in visitor spaces properly recorded in the Visitor and Vehicle Log?

Does the security technician or security officer conduct at least one documented, randomly timed check of the vehicles in the parking lot each working day?

Source: Personal communication with Frank LaMorte, Director of Corporate Security, Advo, Inc., March 31, 2005.

TABLE 2-16 Pre-Employment Screening

Do the Human Resources records on all of the last five regular Advo employees hired show that each of the following checks was properly completed before hire?

Verification of right to work in the United States.

Five years comprehensive past employment or up to three years past employment verification.

(continues)

TABLE 2-16 Pre-Employment Screening *(continued)*

Social security check.

Criminal history check for all jurisdictions of residence within the last seven years.

Sex offender registry checks (if applicable).

Department of motor vehicle checks (for sales and positions that require use of company vehicles only).

Do the Human Resources records on all of the last three regular salaried Advo employees hired show that each of the following checks was completed prior to hire?

Verification of the highest level of education referenced.

Credential verification for items that are factors in the hiring decision.

Do Human Resources records on the last five regular Advo employees hired show that the required ten-panel drug screen was completed within seventy-two hours of offer acceptance?

Were all of the ten randomly selected Advo employees hired since the last audit hired in full compliance with the decision making guidelines in the Pre-employment Screening Policy?

Were documented inquiries made into any gaps in employment shown on the applications of the ten randomly selected employees?

Source: Personal communication with Frank LaMorte, Director of Corporate Security, Advo, Inc., March 31, 2005.

TABLE 2-17 Record Access and Retention

Are personnel files stored securely and accessible only by authorized employees?

Are backup tapes stored in a media-rated fire safe?

Source: Personal communication with Frank LaMorte, Director of Corporate Security, Advo, Inc., March 31, 2005.

TABLE 2-18 Security Cameras

Are security cameras installed at this facility?

Are all cameras fully operational?

Are cameras in place at each of the following required locations?

Roof-mounted color pan, tilt and zoom camera with auto iris and effective low light performance at each building corner.

Main entrance exterior door.

Employee entrance exterior door.

Trucker's entrance exterior door.

Truck gate.

Employee parking area gate.

On each side of the transportation office monitoring shipping/receiving areas.

On each exterior wall of the warehouse looking toward the transportation office monitoring shipping/receiving areas.

Inside the reception area above the reception desk monitoring the visitor lobby.

Do all cameras produce recorded images useful for investigation and identification purposes?

Is each digital video recorder equipped with an uninterruptible power supply?

Is a keyboard-video-monitor device in place for each digital video recorder?

Is each keyboard-video-monitor automatically updating antivirus definitions via the automated corporate system?

Source: Personal communication with Frank LaMorte, Director of Corporate Security, Advo, Inc., March 31, 2005.

TABLE 2-19 Security Incident Reporting

Were all security incidents that occurred reported?

Were all of the incidents reported to the SCC within fifteen minutes of discovery by an employee?

Did the responsible employee submit a completed Security Incident Report on each incident to the Security Manager within twenty-four hours?

Source: Personal communication with Frank LaMorte, Director of Corporate Security, Advo, Inc., March 31, 2005.

TABLE 2-20 Security Officers and Technicians

Is a security associate working full time at this facility?

Does the security associate consistently monitor the facility for issues and take proper action when they are encountered?

Does the security associate or a designated member of the management team effectively diagnose and troubleshoot user-level card access, intrusion alarm, and closed circuit television system issues at the facility?

Does the security associate provide effective 24–7 response to security and emergency incidents?

Does the security associate consistently participate in Safety Committee meetings?

Does the security associate consistently submit all required reports on time?

Does the security associate consistently maintain all required records?

Is the security associate viewed as an active and valued partner by the management team?

Does the security technician have an active liaison with a ranking member of the local police department?

Does the security technician have an active liaison with a ranking member of the local fire department?

(continues)

TABLE 2-20 Security Officers and Technicians *(continued)*

Does the security technician have an active liaison with a ranking member of the local emergency medical service?

Does the security technician or manager have an active liaison with a ranking member of the Department of Homeland Security?

Does the security technician or manager have an active liaison with the USPS Postal Inspector responsible for the area?

Source: Personal communication with Frank LaMorte, Director of Corporate Security, Advo, Inc., March 31, 2005.

TABLE 2-21 Tour Management System

Does a security associate conduct a minimum of two interior and two exterior tours using the Tiscor Tour Management System every day?

Does a review of at least ten randomly selected tours show that the tours are consistently completed properly?

Source: Personal communication with Frank LaMorte, Director of Corporate Security, Advo, Inc., March 31, 2005.

TABLE 2-22 Utility Security

Do the following utilities enter the facility underground or as high as possible on the building? Electricity, telephone, data.

Source: Personal communication with Frank LaMorte, Director of Corporate Security, Advo, Inc., March 31, 2005.

TABLE 2-23 Workplace Violence

Were any criminal incidents referred to police for investigation?

If pre-indicators of violence were present, were they reported when they were observed in accordance with the policy?

Was disciplinary action taken against any employee who engaged in threats, threatening conduct, or any other act of aggression or violence?

Were all situations regarding protective or restraining orders brought to the attention of management by the employee before an incident occurred?

Source: Personal communication with Frank LaMorte, Director of Corporate Security, Advo, Inc., March 31, 2005.

Endnotes

1. U.S. Securities and Exchange Commission, Form 10-K, "Annual Report for the Year Ended September 25, 2004, Advo, Inc." Available: http://www.sec.gov/Archives/edgar/data/801622/000095012304014600/y69370e10vk.txt.

2. Advo, Inc., "About Advo: Corporate Citizenship." Available: http://www.advo.com/corpcitizenship.html.

3. Personal communication with Frank LaMorte, Director of Corporate Security, and Philip McMurray, Director, IT Security and Enterprise Architecture, Advo, Inc., March 17, 2005.

4. Prior to 1997, IBM Global Services was called Integrated Systems Solutions Corporation.

5. Rachael Bell wrote an interesting and detailed chronology of the 2001 U.S. Anthrax attacks entitled, "Amerithrax: An objective look at the unsuccessful FBI investigation of the 2001 anthrax attack." See Court TV's Crime Library website, http://www.crimelibrary.com/terrorists_spies/terrorists/anthrax/index.html?sect=22.

6. There are different forms of anthrax infection. Inhalation anthrax infects the respiratory tract and is more deadly than cutaneous anthrax, which infects the skin. The U.S. Centers for Disease Control and Prevention website provides a wealth of information: http://www.bt.cdc.gov/agent/anthrax/faq/index.asp.

7. Centers for Disease Control and Prevention, "Update: Investigation of Bioterrorism-Related Anthrax and Adverse Events from Antimicrobial Prophylaxis." November 9, 2001. Available: http://www.cdc.gov/mmwr/preview/mmwrhtml/mm5044a1.htm.

8. United States Postal Service, "A Message to Americans from the United States Postal Service." October 19, 2001. Available: http://www.usps.com/news/2001/press/pr01_1019postcard.htm.

9. U.S. Securities and Exchange Commission, Form 10-K, "Annual Report for the Year Ended September 29, 2001, Advo, Inc." Available: http://www.sec.gov/Archives/edgar/data/801622/000092701601504260/d10k.txt.

10. Personal communication with Frank LaMorte, Director of Corporate Security, and Philip McMurray, Director of IT Security and Enterprise Architecture, Advo, Inc., March 31, 2005.

11. Statement on Auditing Standards (SAS) No. 70, "What is ISO 17799? What is BS 7799?" Available: http://www.sas70.com/faq/faq15.html.

12. SAS 70 dot com, "About SAS 70." Available: http://www.sas70.com/about.htm.

13. Tiscor. Available: http://www.tiscor.com.

14. U.S. Securities and Exchange Commission, Form 10-K, "2002 Annual Report, Advo, Inc." Available: http://www.sec.gov/Archives/edgar/data/801622/000095012302011744/y66268exv13.txt.

15. By the end of 2003, the title of the Senior Vice President of Security Management had been changed to Senior Vice President of Safety & Security, and then to Senior Vice President of Security. See U.S. Securities and Exchange Commission, Form 10-K, "Annual Report for the Year Ended September 28, 2002, Advo, Inc." Available:

http://www.sec.gov/Archives/edgar/data/801622/000095012302011744/ y66268e10vk.txt. See also U.S. Securities and Exchange Commission, Form 10-K, "Annual Report for the Year Ended September 27, 2003, Advo, Inc." Available: http://www.sec.gov/Archives/ edgar/data/801622/000095012303013972/y92342e10vk.txt.

16. Advo purchased the CCure 800 System from Software House. Details and specifications can be found at http://www.swhouse.com/ products/software_CCURE800.aspx.

17. Strohl Systems, Business Continuity Planning Software, LDRPS. Available: http://www.strohlsystems.com/Software/LDRPS/default.asp.

18. *Dark hours* describes the state of a building during late night hours, when there are no operations occurring and the building is unoccupied. During dark hours, the building is monitored by the SCC at corporate headquarters.

CASE STUDY QUESTIONS

1. Traditionally, managing IT security and physical security have been treated as two separate domains. Why should they be integrated?

2. Why is top management's awareness and support essential for establishing and maintaining security?

3. Why should those responsible for leading the organization's security efforts be placed high in the organizational chart?

4. The first decision made by Advo's top management in the aftermath of the 9/11 attacks was to improve physical security. Why was attention focused on this particular aspect of security?

5. What are the advantages and disadvantages of using consultants and third-party organizations to provide security-related services? What reasons would a company have for hiring consultants to provide guidance for its security efforts?

6. Why is it a good security practice to have few visitors in a reception area?

7. Identify the security risks involved in allowing networked systems to be used by large numbers of temporary employees who do not need to log in. What password guidelines should be implemented for stronger user authentication?

8. How far away should a backup site be located from company headquarters? What factors should be considered in determining the location of a backup site?

9. Advo believes that frequent audits help to ingrain a security mindset among the company's employees. What other benefits are there to performing frequent security audits?

10. The vendor of Advo's security management system is Software House. Research the role of Software House in the Open Security Exchange (OSE). What is the purpose of the OSE?

KEY TERMS

British Standard 7799 (BS7799): Code of practice for establishing an information security management system. It was first published by the National Standards Body of the United Kingdom in 1995. It establishes guidelines for information security controls, and it consists of two parts. Part I provides a detailed and comprehensive list of good security practices. Part II summarizes the security controls and provides specifications for an information security management system. In 2000, Part I was published as International Organization for Standardization/International Electrotechnical Commission (ISO/IEC) 17799.

Demilitarized Zone (DMZ): Subnetwork that sits between a trusted, internal network and an untrusted, external network.

Firewall: Hardware device, software application, or combination of both that filters the traffic passing between a protected network and an unprotected network.

Intrusion Detection System (IDS): Software used to monitor and analyze system resource use or network traffic patterns. It issues alerts when it detects attempted or successful attacks to gain unauthorized access.

Intrusion Prevention System (IPS): A more advanced form of an IDS that can more accurately differentiate real attacks from false alarms.

Kiosk PC: Stand-alone structure that houses a microcomputer and is located in a public area.

Mantrap: Double-door facility in which an individual's identity must be verified before the individual is allowed to proceed. Failure to provide proof of identity results in the individual remaining trapped between the double doors until security officers arrive.

Opt-in: A program that allows the individual the choice of participating.

Physical Security: Use of locks, guards, badges, alarms, and other physical measures to protect personnel, prevent unauthorized access to facilities, equipment, or other assets, and protect them from sabotage, damage, or theft.

Redundancy: Duplication of equipment and processing capabilities so that the secondary system can assume operations in the event that the primary system fails.

Role-Based Access Control (RBAC): Access control method in which system access is restricted to authorized users whose permissions are assigned according to their job functions.

Server Farm: Collection of computer servers networked and housed in one location. Computer processing is distributed between the individual servers. Load-balancing software is used to track the demand for processing power from different machines and to prioritize and schedule processing tasks. It typically has a primary server and a backup server dedicated to a particular task, so that if the primary server fails, the backup server continues processing.

Shared Mail: Advertisements and other types of mail that are combined from different businesses and distributed at the same time to the intended recipients.

Solo Mailer: Company that sends out advertisements and other types of mail for individual clients. The intended recipients and the timing of delivery are determined by each client.

Spyware: Computer program that surreptitiously gathers and reports information about the use of a computer, without the user's knowledge or consent.

Statement on Auditing Standards 70 (SAS 70): Auditing standard developed by the American Institute of Certified Public Accountants. It is used by independent auditors to formally review and evaluate a service organization's control activities and processes.

Terabyte: A measure of computer storage capacity that is equal to approximately one trillion bytes.

Uninterruptible Power Supply (UPS): Device located between a power supply and a computer that helps to ensure continued computer operation in the event of unexpected voltage fluctuations or power failures.

Virtual Private Network (VPN): Trusted, encrypted connection that occurs over a public network.

YALE NEW HAVEN CENTER FOR EMERGENCY PREPAREDNESS AND DISASTER RESPONSE:

CONTINGENCY PLANNING

Contingency planning allows an organization to be prepared for the unexpected. It involves a variety of complex and intricate activities, among them identifying possible crisis situations and their impacts, managing the organization's level of risk, determining appropriate responses to different circumstances, clearly identifying individual responsibilities, coordinating necessary personnel from all critical areas, establishing leadership during the crisis, training all parties for consistent understanding of procedures and terminology, providing for the availability of necessary resources, ensuring that up-to-date information can be communicated between internal personnel and external organizations and agencies, and establishing recurring drills and exercises. Contingency planning is crucial to the viability of any organization. In a medical environment, preparing for emergencies and planning for disaster response also are essential for the survival of untold numbers of individuals.

This case study describes the disaster planning initiatives, education and training programs, clinical strategies, and logistical solutions developed by the Yale New Haven Center for Emergency Preparedness and Disaster Response. To provide necessary background information, the case study begins with an overview of the Yale New Haven Health System and the Yale New Haven Center for Emergency Preparedness and Disaster Response.

Yale New Haven Health System

Established in 1983, the Yale New Haven Health System (YNHHS) is the largest and most comprehensive integrated healthcare delivery system in Connecticut.[1] YNHHS serves more than 76,000 patient admissions and 642,000 outpatient and emergency visits each year. It provides more than 1,500 beds, employs a support staff of more than 11,000, and has more than 2,800 physicians and 670 residents practicing in more than 200 medical specialties.[2,3,4]

YNHHS is composed of three corporate members: Yale New Haven Network Corporation, Bridgeport Hospital and Healthcare, Inc., and Greenwich Health Care Services, Inc. Through its corporate members, YNHHS operates three large hospitals and numerous affiliate organizations. These are diagrammed in Figure 3-1.

Yale New Haven Network Corporation is the parent company of Yale-New Haven Hospital. Located in New Haven, Connecticut, Yale-New Haven Hospital was founded in 1826. It was Connecticut's first, and the nation's fifth, hospital. Today, Yale-New Haven Hospital is the largest acute care provider in southern Connecticut and the flagship provider for YNHHS. The 944-bed hospital, which includes the Yale-New Haven Children's Hospital and the Yale-New Haven Psychiatric Hospital, maintains a primary affiliation with the Yale University School

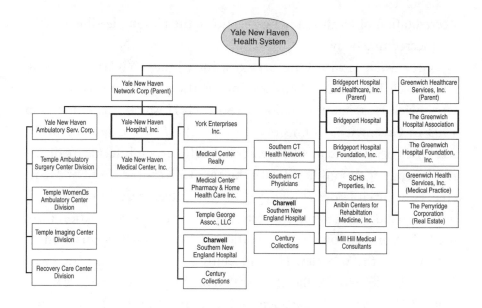

FIGURE 3-1 Yale New Haven Health System Organizational Chart.
Source: "Annual Report on the Financial Status of Connecticut's Short Term Acute Care Hospitals for Fiscal Year 2003," Prepared by the State of Connecticut Office of Health Care Access, February 2005. Available: http://www.ct.gov/ohca/lib/ohca/publications/fsreport_2005.pdf.

of Medicine. Yale-New Haven Hospital is one of fifty medical centers in the United States that collectively train nearly forty percent of the nation's medical residents each year.[5] The hospital is a major referral center throughout the world, and for more than a decade, it has been ranked as one of the best hospitals in the United States.[6]

Bridgeport Hospital and Healthcare, Inc. joined YNHHS in 1996. Bridgeport Hospital and Healthcare, Inc., is the parent company of Bridgeport Hospital. Established in Bridgeport, Connecticut, in 1878, Bridgeport Hospital was Connecticut's third hospital.[7] Today, the 425-bed comprehensive healthcare facility operates its own School of Nursing and is a major affiliate of the Yale University School of Medicine. Bridgeport Hospital is among the top five percent of hospitals in the United States to receive the highest level of accreditation from the Joint Commission on

Accreditation of Healthcare Organizations, the nation's leading health-care accrediting body.[8]

Greenwich Health Care Services, Inc., joined YNHHS in 1998. Greenwich Health Care Services, Inc., is the parent company of the Greenwich Hospital Association. Greenwich Hospital was founded in 1903 in Greenwich, Connecticut. Today, the 174-bed not-for-profit teaching hospital and medical center has a three-year internal medicine residency program affiliated with the Yale University School of Medicine. Greenwich Hospital is among the top fifteen percent of hospitals in the United States to receive accreditation with commendation from the Joint Commission on Accreditation of Healthcare Organizations.[9]

In 2001, the Yale New Haven Health System was designated as a Center of Excellence for Bioterrorism Preparedness and Response by the State of Connecticut Department of Public Health (DPH). As a Center of Excellence, YNHHS provides a leadership role in regional coordination, education, clinical care, and research to improve Connecticut's ability to respond to a large-scale bioterrorism event.[10] In this capacity, YNHHS works with the DPH to develop better ways to monitor and detect biological and chemical incidents, to assess the ability of Connecticut hospitals to provide emergency services, and to improve the communication and notification systems within the state's emergency management network.[11] To coordinate YNHHS' response to terrorist acts, and to support its DPH-designation as a Center of Excellence, the Yale New Haven Center for Emergency Preparedness and Disaster Response was established.

Yale New Haven Center for Emergency Preparedness and Disaster Response

Following the September 11, 2001 terrorist attacks, the President and CEO of YNHHS requested an evaluation of emergency and terrorism preparedness activities at Yale-New Haven Hospital, Bridgeport Hospital, and Greenwich Hospital. This action led to the creation of the Yale

New Haven Center for Emergency Preparedness and Disaster Response, which was established by YNHHS in June 2002. Its mission is to develop and deliver services that improve healthcare planning, preparedness, and response for emergency events and disasters.[12] In accordance with this mission, the center's initiatives are targeted toward five objectives: to identify the status of emergency preparedness within the YNHHS member hospitals; to prepare YNHHS to respond effectively to emergency preparedness and disaster response issues; to provide leadership to healthcare delivery organizations (e.g., acute care hospitals, skilled nursing facilities, community health centers, home health agencies, urgent care centers, emergency medical service providers, and community medical practices) and their workforce regarding emergency preparedness and disaster response issues; to serve as a model for emergency preparedness and disaster response initiatives at the national and international levels; and to advise statewide and national legislative and nongovernmental organizations on the development of standards and policies for emergency preparedness and disaster response in healthcare delivery organizations.[13]

To help the center achieve its objectives, three committees were established (Figure 3-2). The Executive Committee consists of senior administrative and medical personnel from each of the YNHHS member hospitals. It offers support and advice to the center and oversees the System Emergency Preparedness Committee and the System Clinical Advisory Committee. The System Emergency Preparedness Committee is responsible for developing the operational elements of emergency preparedness and response. Its members are representatives of information services, telecommunications, patient care services, laboratory services, pharmacy, materials management, facility management, security, and education. The System Clinical Advisory Committee is responsible for developing medical diagnostic and treatment guidelines for hospital emergency response. Its members are physician experts in infectious disease,

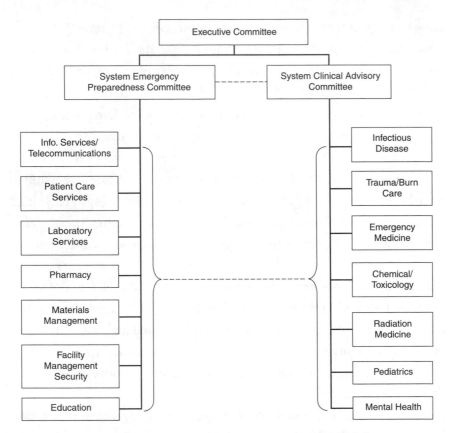

FIGURE 3-2 Committee Structure, Yale New Haven Center for Emergency Preparedness and Disaster Response.

Source: Christopher M. Cannon, Director, Center for Emergency Preparedness and Disaster Response, Yale New Haven Health System, June 10, 2005.

trauma, burn care, emergency medicine, chemical/toxicology, radiation medicine, pediatrics and mental health.[13]

The center is supported by the administrative, operational, and clinical expertise of YNHHS. Based on this support and partnerships developed at the local, state, and national levels,[12] the center has developed detailed plans and practical procedures for emergency preparedness and disaster response. Its programs and services are in four distinct areas: disaster planning, education and training, clinical strategies, and logistical solutions.

Disaster Planning

The Yale New Haven Center for Emergency Preparedness and Disaster Response has been the leader of a number of emergency planning initiatives within YNHHS, the State of Connecticut, the Northeast, the nation, and the international community.

Disaster Planning: YNHHS

Within the YNHHS, the Center for Emergency Preparedness and Disaster Response has implemented a Hospital Emergency Incident Command System (HEICS) at Yale-New Haven Hospital, Bridgeport Hospital, and Greenwich Hospital. The HEICS establishes an organizational structure that is used to command, control, and coordinate emergency response efforts during a disaster (Figure 3-3). The HEICS builds on a previously existing model for incident command systems for hospital emergency management by expanding the responsibilities of the Incident Commander and adding eight leadership positions (highlighted in gray in Figure 3-3).[14]

The HEICS is activated upon official declaration of a disaster such as a terrorism-related attack, a mass casualty incident, or a chemical, biological, radiological, or nuclear emergency. The HEICS operates under the authority of an Incident Commander, typically a senior-level hospital administrator. It is the Incident Commander's responsibility to assess the extent of the emergency, determine the ability of the YNHHS hospitals to respond, identify the personnel who are needed, assign and coordinate staff emergency activities, distribute specific instructions to all HEICS team members, and remain apprised of all critical events that transpire during the crisis situation. The HEICS remains operational until it is deactivated by the Incident Commander.[15]

Other members of the HEICS Command Section staff are the Public Information Officer (who updates the media, staff, and visitors about the incident), the Safety and Security Officer (who assesses the hazards

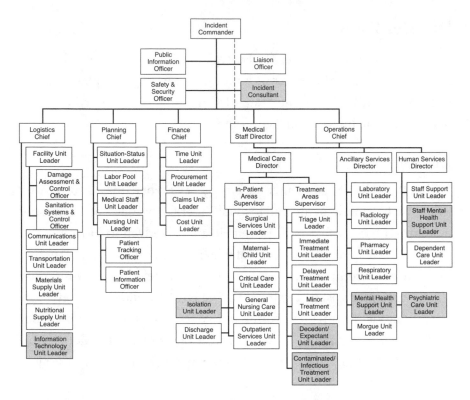

FIGURE 3-3   Hospital Emergency Incident Command System (HEICS) organizational chart.

Source: Christopher M. Cannon, Director, Center for Emergency Preparedness and Disaster Response, Yale New Haven Health System, June 10, 2005.

and helps to ensure the safety of personnel), the Liaison Officer (who communicates with government agencies and other organizations), and the Incident Consultant (who provides specialized medical, environmental or legal expertise to the Incident Commander).[15] The general staff of the HEICS consists of four sections: Logistics, Planning, Finance, and Operations. Each section is headed by a chief.[15]

The Logistics Section manages the materials and facilities used during an emergency.[15] Included in this section is the Information Technology Unit Leader, who provides static information (e.g., employee contact information) and dynamic information (e.g., situation status reports) to hospital emergency responders. The Information Technology Unit Leader also supports internal and external electronic communication capabilities.[14] The Planning Section determines the resources that are needed during an emergency and establishes the action plans required for incident response.[15] The Finance Section tracks and manages hospital spending during a crisis, including emergency capital expenditures and claims reimbursements.[15]

The Operations Section provides the medical services required during an emergency. Included in this section are the Isolation Unit Leader (who coordinates the medical management of infectious patients), the Decedent/Expectant Unit Leader (who coordinates the management of patients who are dead on arrival, die during treatment, or are expected to die imminently), the Contaminated/Infectious Treatment Unit Leader (who coordinates the management of contaminated/infectious patients, including patient triage, assessment, resuscitation, and decontamination), two Mental Health Support Leaders and a Psychiatric Care Unit Leader (who coordinate the mental health support for patients, guests, hospital healthcare workers and dependents).[14]

Disaster Planning: State of Connecticut

Within the State of Connecticut, the center has helped to develop a regional emergency planning process among the state's 32 acute care hospitals, 180 emergency medical service agencies, 45 community health centers, 30,000 community medical practitioners, 45 urgent care centers, 200 skilled nursing facilities, 86 home health agencies, 96 local public health agencies, and 14 local mental health authorities.[13] These healthcare delivery organizations are organized into five emergency planning regions (Figure 3-4) to help build healthcare capacity and to provide a coordinated response to acts of terrorism and other medical-related emergencies. This integrated planning approach to emergency preparedness is endorsed as a national model by the Joint Commission on Accreditation of Healthcare Organizations.[12]

In collaboration with the DPH, the center has identified each health-care delivery organization's role and the emergency preparedness critical capacities (e.g., programs and services) needed to fulfill that role. Based on the identified critical capacities, the center conducted needs assessments for each healthcare organization in the areas of education and training (including courses, drills and exercises), clinical strategies (including laboratory testing and medical stockpiling), and logistical solutions (including emergency credentialing, surge capacity, and risk/crisis communication).[13] The center's review of the needs assessments identified gaps in emergency preparedness. These gaps are being addressed by new programs and services developed by the center (described in the following sections), as well as by the adaptation of existing programs and services offered by the individual healthcare organizations.

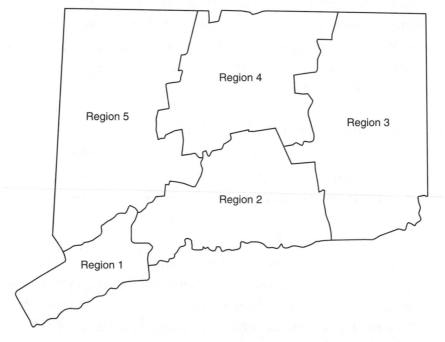

FIGURE 3-4　The five Connecticut emergency public health preparedness planning regions.

Source: State of Connecticut Department of Mental Health and Addiction Services. Available: http://www.dmhas.state.ct.us/.

The center also works with Connecticut's professional health associations to coordinate initiatives and to share best practice ideas in regional planning, education and training, clinical strategies, and logistical solutions. Among its partners are the Connecticut Hospital Association, the Connecticut Area Health Education Centers, the Connecticut Association of Health Care Facilities, the Connecticut Association for Home Care, the Connecticut Association of Not-for-Profit Providers for the Aging, the Connecticut Association of Directors of Health, the Connecticut Nurses' Association, the Connecticut Primary Care Association, the Connecticut Society of Health-System Pharmacists, the Connecticut Society of Radiologic Technologists, the Connecticut Society for Respiratory Care, and the Connecticut State Medical Society.[16]

In addition to its partnerships with the DPH and the state's many healthcare organizations and associations, the center works with Connecticut's Department of Public Safety/Division of Homeland Security, Office of Emergency Management, and Office of Policy and Management to coordinate the needs and capabilities of the state's healthcare organizations with the emergency planning and response processes established by state government.[16]

Disaster Planning: Regional, National, and International

Beyond the State of Connecticut, the center works with healthcare delivery organizations and governments throughout the Northeast to develop a coordinated approach for regional emergency preparedness. The center routinely shares its emergency preparedness and disaster response education and training materials with the Maryland Department of Public Health, the Rhode Island Department of Health, and the Vermont Department of Health. The center also participates in the Tri-State Metro Bioterrorism Work Group, in conjunction with the New Jersey Department of Health and the New York State Department of Health.[16]

On the national level, the center works with several federal agencies and organizations to develop emergency management standards and programs. The center is a member of the Community-Based Emergency Management Roundtable national standards working group, which operates under the auspices of the Joint Commission on Accreditation of Healthcare Organizations.[13] The center also is a member of the Homeland Security/Defense Education Consortium, an institutional network established by the North American Aerospace Defense Command and the U.S. Northern Command to promote homeland security–related education and research. In partnership with both the American Medical Association and the Health Resources and Services Administration (HRSA) of the U.S Department of Health and Human Services, the center helps to provide emergency preparedness education and training to the nation's healthcare delivery workforce. It also participates in the HRSA national working group to develop an electronic system for advance registration of volunteer health professionals.[13] In association with the American Society for Testing and Materials, the center participates in establishing national standards for emergency preparedness in healthcare delivery organizations. Additionally, the center works with the U.S. Department of Homeland Security to evaluate the content of the nation's healthcare education and training curricula.[13]

On the international level, the center works with the Pan American Health Organization, the World Association for Disaster and Emergency Medicine, and the World Health Organization. Through these associations, the center's education and training programs for emergency preparedness are adapted and disseminated throughout the world.[17]

Education and Training

In 2002, the DPH contracted with the center to provide education and training in emergency preparedness and disaster response to the 178,500 healthcare delivery workers throughout Connecticut.[18] The goal was clear: The center needed to provide a fundamental level of emergency management awareness to a large, diverse, and geographically dispersed workforce employed by many different types of healthcare delivery organizations (hospitals, emergency medical service agencies, community health centers, medical practitioner offices, urgent care centers, skilled nursing facilities, home health agencies, mental health authorities, and public health agencies). Less clear were the emergency preparedness educational needs of these organizations, the associated knowledge levels of their employees, and the adaptability of existing courses.

As part of its disaster planning initiatives, the center conducted needs assessments in education and training for each healthcare organization. Surveys were conducted to identify the healthcare delivery workers' level of education in emergency preparedness and disaster response, as well as their training preferences. The center conducted a literature review and researched existing courses to determine their applicability to the target audience.[18] The center also collaborated with Columbia University and St. Louis University to evaluate existing emergency preparedness curricula.[12] The results were used to develop courses that are adaptable for different healthcare organizations.

The courses use common terminology to promote communication between healthcare workers and to enable an integrated response during an emergency.[18] They are free and are accessible through the center's Online Education and Training website, http://ynhhs.emergencyeducation.org/. The courses also are available on CD-ROM and video. The center currently offers two introductory courses that target a broad range of disciplines and skill levels:

- *Emergency Management 102: Introductory Course* (EM 102) offers awareness-level emergency preparedness training for the healthcare delivery workforce. This course helps healthcare workers to understand the consequences of emergencies and disasters, and it assists them in preparing for their responsibilities during an emergency or terrorist event. In addition to providing a basic program in emergency management, EM 102 includes information on addressing mental health needs during an emergency.[19]

■ *Incident Command Systems* (ICS) *for Health Care* (EM 140) introduces healthcare workers to the concept of an incident command system. The course describes the ways in which an ICS can assist in the command, control, and coordination of all response efforts during an emergency. It discusses the composition of an ICS and it provides an overview of the members' roles and responsibilities. The course also reviews the purpose of a unified command, which enables multiple organizations with different responsibilities to interact effectively during a wide-scale emergency.[19]

Additional courses are in the process of being developed by the center. Three courses are expected to be available in the near future:

■ *Introduction to Personal Protective Equipment, Infection Control and Decontamination* (EM 120) will provide introductory-level information about personal protective equipment, infection control practices, and decontamination procedures that are needed to ensure the safety of healthcare workers and patients during an emergency.[20]

■ *Bioterrorism Preparedness for Clinicians* (EM 201) is an intermediate-level course that will help physicians and other medical practitioners to recognize bioterrorism agent disease syndromes, learn the necessary precautions, and understand their roles in the event of a public health emergency.[20]

■ *Mental Health Aspects of Emergencies and Disasters for Non-Mental Health Professionals* (EM 230) is an intermediate-level course that will help medical practitioners to assess and to respond to the immediate mental health needs of patients affected by emergencies or disasters. It also will offer recommendations to ensure healthcare worker safety during these events.[20]

An important part of the center's education and training strategy is its ability to assess the effectiveness of its courses. The center has developed a number of tabletop exercises based on realistic biological, chemical, and radiological scenarios. It also has developed and coordinated a series of full functional drills and exercises that support emergency preparedness planning at the three YNHHS hospitals.[12] The center uses these drills and exercises to measure how well course content is translated into action during a simulated disaster, and to update the courses as needed to improve effectiveness. The drills and exercises also are used to increase the practical skills of the participating individuals and the overall competencies of the contributing organizations. In addition, the drills and exercises are used to ensure that the plans and procedures used by multiple regional response organizations (e.g., public safety, public health, emergency medical services, and government agencies) are fully integrated.[13]

Clinical Strategies

The center has contributed to the development of numerous clinical strategies for disaster response. Through its association with national- and world-renowned physician experts at YNHHS, protocols have been developed and communicated to healthcare practitioners throughout Connecticut. Many of the center's plans and protocols focus on chemical, biological, and radiological emergencies.

The Connecticut Hospital Chemical Response Plan was created to address the antidotes, decontamination procedures, and surge capacities that are needed to respond to a chemical event.[21] This plan was developed for use by YNHHS clinical experts as a statewide acute care hospital chemical response model.[12]

A Universal Respiratory Etiquette protocol was designed to reduce the spread of easily transmissible and contagious diseases, and to reduce the risks of transmitting infections among and between patients, medical personnel, staff, and others with whom contact is possible. This protocol has been implemented in all of Connecticut's acute care hospitals, emergency medical service agencies, and outpatient service areas.[12]

Specific infection control protocols have been developed for influenza, smallpox, and severe acute respiratory syndrome. To help other healthcare organizations develop their own plans, the center developed an Infectious Disease Control Protocol Flowchart template that outlines every aspect of infection control, including case definition, the use of personal protective equipment, environmental controls, and visitation policies.[12]

The Connecticut Hospital Radiation Response Plan was created to identify the decontamination, triage, and treatment resources that should be mobilized after the occurrence of a radiation event. This plan is being considered as a model for implementation by other states.[12]

The center has collaborated with the DPH to develop a biodosimetry laboratory to evaluate and manage the health risks associated with radiation exposure. This laboratory is one of only three such laboratories in the nation that focus on the biological assessment of radiation exposure.[22] The laboratory is used to provide timely information to healthcare delivery personnel about patient radiation exposure. It also is being used to support the development of new methods for calculating individual radiation exposure so that larger numbers of people can be screened in the aftermath of a terrorist-related radiological event.[22]

The center also has worked with the DPH to develop an implementation plan for a hospital emergency department syndromic surveillance program. This program, which enables the early detection of terrorism-related illnesses, analyzes health-related data from hospital emergency departments to identify trends in symptoms that are consistent with biological, chemical, or radiation exposure.[12] The data can be used to more quickly detect outbreaks, estimate the immediate impact of the disease, determine the rate of distribution and spread of the illness, and facilitate necessary control measures. Data analysis is an important aspect of this program, and the center has played a key role in evaluating existing syndromic surveillance software products for use in Connecticut's hospitals.

Logistical Solutions

The center has played a significant role in the development of disaster recovery plans to protect the healthcare infrastructure within YNHHS and the state of Connecticut. Several initiatives have been implemented to ensure that there will be sufficient medical personnel, facilities, equipment, and supplies to effectively respond to a disaster and to ensure that the emergency communication systems will function accurately and reliably throughout the crisis.

Medical Personnel

The center has established a volunteer Medical Reserve Corps[23] unit to support the personnel needs of Connecticut hospitals during a disaster. The specially trained volunteers include clinical practitioners (physicians, physician assistants, nurses, pharmacists, pharmacy technicians, diagnostic imaging professionals, dentists, respiratory therapists, clinical laboratory practitioners, mental health practitioners, and paramedics); students currently enrolled in the School of Medicine and the School of Public Health at Yale University; and retired medical professionals. During a large-scale emergency, the Medical Reserve Corps volunteers will work collaboratively with other medical personnel and public health professionals to supplement the state's existing emergency response resources.

As part of the Medical Reserve Corps, the center has developed and implemented a statewide emergency credentialing program. This program, developed in partnership with several state agencies and healthcare professional associations in Connecticut,[24] provides a way for hospitals to contact Medical Reserve Corps volunteers during a disaster and to be sure that these individuals are qualified to offer assistance. Healthcare professionals who are interested in joining the Medical Reserve Corps must provide certain information to the center, including name, academic degree, hospital affiliation, medical specialty, state license number, date of last appointment, home telephone number, beeper number, cell phone number, and office telephone number.[25] Specific capabilities and qualifications are verified by the individual's healthcare delivery organization before the information is entered into a centralized database. The database is administered by the center and is accessible by all of Connecticut's acute care hospitals during a disaster. The Joint Commission on Accreditation of Healthcare Organizations has endorsed the center's emergency credentialing program as a national model.[12]

Facilities

Critically ill patients typically go directly to the emergency rooms of local hospitals for treatment. Hospitals are first responders during times of crisis, and they need sufficient capacity to be able to treat the sudden surge and continuing deluge of critically ill patients during a disaster. According to guidelines established by the Health Resources and Services Administration, there should be 500 hospital beds available for every 1,000,000 people. There are approximately 3,400,000 people in Connecticut; therefore, the state needs to have 1,700 hospital beds available at any time.[17] Unfortunately, Connecticut hospitals do not have this excess capacity. There are a total of 7,152 hospital beds in Connecticut and the occupancy rate typically exceeds 76%.[26]

To address the need for increased facilities during a disaster, the center assisted with the development of the administrative and operational protocols for staffing, equipping and managing a Mobile and Surge Hospital (MaSH).[12] The 100-bed portable hospital can be deployed in twenty-five bed increments for use in providing triage and treatment anywhere in the state.[27] The facility resembles a collection of trailers and tents. It can be moved to a site in less than six hours and it can be fully functioning within forty-eight hours. The MaSH contains approximately $3 million worth of medical equipment, has its own generators, and is largely self-contained. The facility also includes space to isolate patients with infectious diseases (e.g., smallpox). In addition to providing additional capacity during a disaster, the MaSH can be used as a training facility for emergency responders throughout the state and the region.[28]

Equipment and Supplies

During the first three days of a major attack or mass casualty event, each hospital must rely primarily on its own equipment and supplies and secondarily on the reserves that can be provided by local healthcare organizations (e.g., other acute care hospitals, emergency medical service agencies, urgent care centers, rehabilitation facilities, community medical practitioners, skilled nursing facilities, community health centers, and local health departments).[13] Depending on the magnitude and duration of the event, Connecticut hospitals may receive additional assistance from state agencies (e.g., the Connecticut DPH, the Connecticut Disaster Medical Assistance Team, the Connecticut Office of Emergency Management, and the Connecticut Division of Homeland Security).[13] Federal resources will be made available if needed, but they are not accessible within the first seventy-two hours of a disaster.[17] If the event involves initial or anticipated mass casualties, the office of the state governor can request the deployment of Strategic National Stockpile (SNS) resources from the Centers for Disease Control and Prevention (CDC). SNS resources will be deployed after the situation has been evaluated by federal officials (those from the CDC and the U.S. Department of Health and Human Services, and possibly those from the U.S. Department of Homeland Security and the U.S. Department of Defense). The SNS is a national depository of life support medications, antibiotics, chemical antidotes, antitoxins, intravenous administration medications, airway maintenance supplies, and medical/surgical items.[29] The first SNS supplies to be made available are twelve-hour Push Packs: collections of pharmaceuticals, antidotes, and medical supplies to treat a variety of illnesses. The packages are so named because they can be delivered to a designated site within twelve hours of the federal decision to deploy. If additional resources are needed, federal vendor managed inventory pharmaceuticals and medical supplies will be shipped for arrival twenty-four to thirty-six hours later.[29]

Because federal resources are not first response tools, the center has worked with the state DPH to coordinate the storage and distribution of equipment, supplies, and pharmaceuticals within and between Connecticut's healthcare delivery organizations. The center developed a Hospital Medical Stockpiling Strategy that integrates planning and makes recommendations about the types and quantities of medical resources that are needed for specific mass casualty events. This stockpiling strategy helps to ensure that Connecticut's hospitals will have sufficient equipment, supplies, and pharmaceuticals during the first seventy-two hours of a disaster to care for their patients.[13] To further enhance response capabilities, the center coordinated the purchase and use of decontamination facilities and personal protective equipment for the state's acute care hospitals and emergency medical service providers.[28]

Emergency Communication Systems

The most common problem in disaster response is poor communication. Communication may be insufficient or incorrect information may be conveyed between first responders. Systems may become overloaded or the communication equipment may fail to work at all.[30]

To improve the quality of communication between the personnel at Yale-New Haven Hospital, Bridgeport Hospital, and Greenwich Hospital, the center implemented the HEICS which is diagrammed in Figure 3-3, and ensures that all staff members know the proper channels of communication, understand their responsibilities, use the same terminology to describe the situation and all response details, and work together in a coordinated manner.[15] The center also established both a primary and a backup (off-site) Emergency Operations Center (EOC) for YNHHS. The EOC is a room where hospital administrators and HEICS leaders meet to discuss the crisis and support the emergency response activities. The EOC is equipped with computers, projectors, copiers, backup power sources, office supplies, plans (floor, building, and evacuation), maps (local, state, and regional), lists (for contacting personnel, vendors, the media, and funeral homes), telephone books (local, state, and regional), and communication devices, including telephones, radios, and fax machines.[15]

To ensure that the communication systems will function when needed, the center helped to establish a statewide communication process between Connecticut's acute care hospitals, the DPH, the State of Connecticut Office of Emergency Management, and the Connecticut Hospital Association.[12] The process incorporates redundancy to improve the reliability of the communication systems.

The acute care hospitals are linked together through a very high frequency (155.340 MHz) radio communication system called MedNet (Medical Network). MedNet also connects the hospitals with the Coordinated Medical Emergency Dispatch centers (CMEDs) located throughout the state. Functioning as communication hubs for the emergency medical service field personnel, the CMEDs use an ultra high frequency (460 MHz) communication system to dispatch and control the location of ambulances and emergency medical service personnel, and to determine the immediate capability of hospitals to accept patients.[31] MedNet is used daily for routine incident coordination purposes. It also is used to coordinate emergency medical resources during a disaster.[32]

In 2004, a satellite-based emergency communication system was established to interconnect Connecticut's acute care hospitals, the DPH, the State of Connecticut Office of Emergency Management and the Connecticut Hospital Association. MedSat (medical satellite) provides users with dedicated telephone and two-way radio communication systems. Using an assigned frequency only available to the emergency response community,[31] MedSat enables all users to communicate reliably over one channel and helps to ensure communication interoperability. Because it functions without relying on existing landlines or commercial electrical power utilities,[32] MedSat also can serve as a backup communication system to the telephone system and to MedNet.

To provide further assurance of communication reliability, the center has evaluated and selected a redundant satellite telephone system for YNHHS. This system fully integrates with the MedSat communication system.[12]

Final Comments

The Yale New Haven Center for Emergency Preparedness and Disaster Response has developed numerous programs and services to improve healthcare planning, emergency preparation, and disaster recovery efforts. Although the center's achievements are remarkable, it continues to plan and develop new initiatives. These include creating additional courses that meet discipline-specific competency standards, recruiting more volunteers for the Medical Reserve Corps, providing additional plans for capacity building, helping to improve the interoperability between medical, police, and fire communication systems, and expanding partnerships at the local, state, and national levels.

Endnotes

1. Yale School of Public Health, "Joseph A. Zaccagnino, President and Chief Executive Officer of Yale-New Haven Hospital and of Yale New Haven Health System, Honored as John D. Thompson Distinguished Visiting Fellow." Available: http://publichealth.yale.edu/news/april05/zaccagnino.html.
2. "About Yale-New Haven Hospital." Available: http://www.ynhh.org/general/general.html.
3. "Bridgeport Hospital, About Us." Available: http://www.bridge-porthospital.org/AboutUs/AboutUs.asp.
4. "Greenwich Hospital's Annual Report 2004." Available: http://www.greenhosp.org/greenwich/ghannual2004.pdf.
5. "Yale-New Haven Delivery Network, Yale-New Haven Hospital." Available: http://yalenewhavenhealth.org/s_members/ynhv.html.

6. "Yale-New Haven Hospital News Release," July 14, 2004. Available: http://www.ynhh.org/press/2004/us_news.html.

7. Yale-New Haven Hospital and Hartford Hospital were the first and second hospitals, respectively, in Connecticut.

8. "Bridgeport Delivery Network, Bridgeport Hospital." Available: http://yalenewhavenhealth.org/s_members/bvn.html.

9. "Greenwich Delivery Network, Greenwich Hospital." Available: http://yalenewhavenhealth.org/s_members/gvn.html#grwhosp.

10. "Yale-New Haven Hospital, Advancing Care, Preparing for the Unthinkable." Available: http://www.ynhh.org/adcare/adcare0602.html.

11. "Yale-New Haven Fall 2002, A Special Report to the Community." Available: http://www.ynhh.org/general/commbenefits02.pdf.

12. Yale New Haven Health, The Yale New Haven Center for Emergency Preparedness and Disaster Response, New Haven, CT, 2004.

13. Christopher M. Cannon, "A Hospital System Approach to Integrating Healthcare Delivery into the Community Emergency Response System." Poster from Christopher M. Cannon, Director, Center for Emergency Preparedness and Disaster Response, Yale New Haven Health System, June 10, 2005.

14. Jeffrey L. Arnold, MD, Louise-Marie Dembry, MD, Ming-Che Tsai, MD, MPH, Ülkümen Rodoplu, MD, Vivek Parwani, MD, James Paturas, EMT-P, Christopher Cannon, FACHE, MPH, Scott Selig, MAT, Joseph Albanese, Ph.D., "Recommended Modifications and Applications of the Hospital Emergency Incident Command System for Hospital Emergency Management Today." Poster from Christopher M. Cannon, Director, Center for Emergency Preparedness and Disaster Response, Yale New Haven Health System, June 10, 2005.

15. "Incident Command Systems (ICS) for Health Care (EM 140)," Yale New Haven Center for Emergency Preparedness and Disaster Response, Online Education and Training. Available: http://ynhhs.emergencyeducation.org/.

16. "Yale New Haven Center for Emergency Preparedness and Disaster Response, Partnerships." Available: http://yalenewhavenhealth.org/emergency/partnerships.html.

17. Personal communication with Christopher M. Cannon, Director, Center for Emergency Preparedness and Disaster Response, Yale New Haven Health System, June 10, 2005.

18. Christopher M. Cannon, "Building Community Emergency Response Capacity through Integrated Healthcare Workforce Education and Training," American Public Health Association 133rd Annual Meeting, November 7, 2005.

19. "Yale New Haven Health, Online Education and Training, Course Descriptions." Available: http://ynhhs.emergencyeducation.org/descriptions.asp.

20. "Yale New Haven Health, Online Education and Training, About Online Education and Training." Available: http://ynhhs.emergencyeducation.org/about.asp.

21. "Yale New Haven Health, Office of Emergency Preparedness, Southern Tier Briefing," April 8, 2004. Available: http://yalenewhavenhealth.org/emergency/commu/briefings/STBriefingV2I15.pdf.

22. "Yale New Haven Center for Emergency Preparedness and Disaster Response, Response Planning." Available: http://yalenewhavenhealth.org/emergency/progsvcs/responseplan.html.

23. The Medical Reserve Corps was established in 2002 as part of Citizen Corps, a national volunteer network to improve homeland security. Citizen Corps is part of the USA Freedom Corps, which promotes volunteer services throughout the nation. The Medical Reserve Corps provides a way of organizing and identifying public health and medical volunteers so that they can provide assistance during a disaster. Additional information can be found at http://www.medicalreservecorps.gov/.

24. The center's emergency credentialing program is provided in partnership with the DPH, the State of Connecticut Department of

Mental Health and Addiction Services, the Connecticut Hospital Association, the Connecticut Association of Medical Staff Services, the Connecticut State Medical Society, the Connecticut Nurses' Association, the Connecticut Society of Health-System Pharmacists, the Connecticut Society of Radiologic Technologists, and the Connecticut Society for Respiratory Care.

25. Richard M. Kleindienst, Sr., Coordinator, Medical Reserve Corps, Yale New Haven Center for Emergency Preparedness and Disaster Response, "Medical Reserve Corps," 2004. Available: http://www.medicalreservecorps.gov/2004Conference/PDF/Richa rd%20M.%20Kleindienst%20Sr.pdf.

26. "Annual Report on the Financial Status of Connecticut's Short Term Acute Care Hospitals for Fiscal Year 2003." Prepared by the State of Connecticut Office of Health Care Access, February 2005. Available: http://www.ct.gov/ohca/lib/ohca/publications/ fsreport_2005.pdf.

27. Cristine A. Vogel, Commissioner, State of Connecticut Office of Health Care Access, November 16, 2004. Available: http://www.ct.gov/ ohca/lib/ohca/condeterminations/04-30398_dtr.pdf.

28. "Yale New Haven Center for Emergency Preparedness and Disaster Response, Capacity Building." Available: http://yalenewhaven health.org/emergency/progsvcs/capacitybuilding.html.

29. "Centers for Disease Control and Prevention, Emergency Preparedness & Response, Strategic National Stockpile." Available: http://www.bt.cdc.gov/stockpile/.

30. "Emergency Management 102: Introductory Course (EM102)," Yale New Haven Center for Emergency Preparedness and Disaster Response, Online Education and Training. Available: http://ynhhs.emergencyeducation.org/.

31. Connecticut Department of Public Health Planning and Preparedness Subcommittee, "Preparedness Planning Guidance for a Regional Response to a Public Health Emergency," April 2004. Available:

http://www.ct.gov/oem/lib/oem/homelandsecurity/joint_dph_oem_regional_planning_guidance.pdf.

32. "State of Connecticut Plan for Enhanced Public Safety Communications Interoperability," February 27, 2004. Available: http://www.ct.gov/oem/lib/oem/docsuploaded/interop_minutes/comm_interop_plan_-_final.pdf.

CASE STUDY QUESTIONS

1. Contingency planning requires an understanding of the crises that are most likely to occur, the potential impacts of those events, the resources that are needed to address those situations, and the most efficient means of accessing those resources. How has the center addressed each of these concerns?

2. The center's contingency planning strategy is based on collaborative partnerships. List the center's local and state partners. What other organizations would you add to this list of partnerships?

3. Why is an integrated planning approach necessary for building healthcare capacity and providing a coordinated response to emergencies and disasters?

4. What is a needs assessment? What role did this play in the center's ability to provide disaster planning, education and training, clinical strategies, and logistical solutions to Connecticut's healthcare delivery infrastructure?

5. What is the difference between a tabletop exercise and a full functional disaster recovery drill? Identify the advantages and disadvantages of each.

6. What is a Hospital Emergency Incident Command System? Identify, and explain the functions of, the five sections of an HEICS. Explain how an HEICS provides unity of command and helps to improve the quality of communication during disaster response.

7. Why are education and training important parts of contingency planning?

8. Why are Strategic National Stockpile resources not available during the first seventy-two hours of a disaster? Why is a coordinated stockpiling strategy better than having each hospital stockpile enough equipment, supplies, and pharmaceuticals to meet its own needs?

9. How does redundancy improve the reliability of communication systems?

10. Why is surge capacity an important element of contingency planning for healthcare delivery organizations?

KEY TERMS

Bioterrorism: The use of biological agents (e.g., bacteria, viruses, toxins) to cause widespread illness or death.

Emergency Operations Center (EOC): Predetermined physical location where the leaders of the Incident Command System/Hospital Emergency Incident Command System meet to discuss the crisis and to support the emergency response activities.

Hospital Emergency Incident Command System (HEICS): Organizational structure used to command, control, and coordinate a hospital's emergency response efforts. Specialized type of Incident Command System.

Incident Commander: Top management position of an Incident Command System or a Hospital Emergency Incident Command System.

Incident Command System (ICS): Organizational structure used to command, control, and coordinate an organization's emergency response efforts.

Joint Commission on Accreditation of Healthcare Organizations: Independent, not-for-profit organization that evaluates the quality of care provided by healthcare organizations. It is the leading healthcare accrediting body in the United States.

Needs Assessment: Systematic study that identifies the requirements of a particular population, defines the extent of those requirements, and helps to identify the actions and resources necessary to fulfill the requirements.

Stockpiling: Accumulating a reserve supply that exceeds present needs in anticipation of a future shortage.

Strategic National Stockpile (SNS): National depository of life support medications, antibiotics, chemical antidotes, antitoxins, intravenous administration medications, airway maintenance supplies, and medical/surgical items. The SNS program is managed by the Centers for Disease Control and Prevention of the U.S. Department of Health and Human Services.

Surge Capacity: Ability to obtain additional resources (e.g., personnel, facilities, equipment, and supplies) when needed during an emergency.

Tabletop Exercise: Form of disaster recovery plan testing in which disaster recovery team members meet to talk through a specific crisis scenario and discuss specific actions they would take to respond to the crisis.

Triage: Process used to categorize sick or injured people according to the severity of their conditions. Allows the patients' needs and treatments to be prioritized so that medical personnel, facilities, equipment, and supplies are used effectively.

Unified Command: Organizational structure that enables multiple organizations with different responsibilities (e.g., fire, police, hospital, emergency medical service units) to interact effectively during a large-scale emergency.

IBM:

THE EMBEDDED SECURITY SUBSYSTEM

I n a network environment, the ability to trust the identities of users and the integrity of systems is critical. Relying on software alone to secure network access points, prevent intruder attacks, or protect sensitive user data is not sufficient. A greater measure of trust is provided when security hardware is integrated within the system architecture. IBM's research on the use of hardware to improve trust led to the development of an integrated security chip known as the Embedded Security Subsystem.

This case study focuses on the Embedded Security Subsystem that IBM developed. It describes the hardware component, outlining its transition from a proprietary chip to one based on open standards, and explaining the means by which it provides strong user authentication and system integrity. To provide necessary background information, the case study begins with an overview of IBM and the Global Security Analysis Lab at the Watson Research Center.

IBM—The Company

IBM was incorporated in New York State on June 16, 1911. At the time of its incorporation, the company was known as the Computing-Tabulating-Recording Company (C-T-R), the result of a merger of the Computing Scale Company of America, the Tabulating Machine Company, and The International Time Recording Company of New York. C-T-R manufactured and sold industrial time recording equipment, commercial scales, meat and cheese slicers, tabulators, and punched cards.[1] In 1924, C-T-R changed its name to International Business Machines Corporation (IBM). The change in name represented a change in the company's focus toward business and technology, and its operations became international.

Today, IBM operates in more than 160 countries worldwide and it derives more than half of its revenues from sales outside of the United States.[2] Headquartered in Armonk, New York, IBM is the largest information technology (IT) company in the world. At the end of 2004, the company had approximately 329,000 employees and its annual revenue exceeded $96.3 billion. IBM also is the world's largest business and technology services company ($46.2 billion in revenue in 2004), and the world's largest financier of IT ($3 billion in revenue in 2004).[3] It is the world's largest IT research organization as well, employing more than 3,000 scientists and engineers at nine laboratories in six countries (Switzerland, China, India, Israel, Japan, and the United States), and investing more than $5.6 billion in IT research in 2004.[4]

IBM has long followed an innovative business model, defining innovation as the intersection of business insight and technological invention. Since 2002, it has focused on computing architecture that exploits network technology. IBM refers to this architecture as the On Demand

Operating Environment: a computer and network infrastructure based on open standards rather than proprietary technologies. These standards have become a core element of IBM's overall strategy.[2]

Abbreviated Organizational Structure

It is a challenge to describe IBM's complex organizational structure. Its size is monolithic, and it plays a dominant role in the global arena of business and technology. Its clients include some of the world's largest organizations, governments, and companies representing every major industry and endeavor.[2] To capitalize on its strengths in IT, business transformation outsourcing, business consulting, systems integration, high-performance hardware, and open enterprise software,[4] IBM has organized its many sectors and activities into a multidimensional organizational structure. What follows is an abbreviated description of this structure.

IBM's operations are organized into six segments: Global Services, Systems and Technology, Software, Global Financing, Enterprise Investments, and Personal Systems.[5]

- *Global Services* includes a number of capabilities, including Business Consulting Services, Business Continuity and Recovery Services, Business Transformation Outsourcing, e-business Hosting Services, support for packaged software and custom and legacy applications, and outsourcing services.[2]
- *Systems and Technology* provides IBM's clients with business solutions requiring advanced computing power and storage capabilities (e.g., eServer and Storage Systems). The group also provides leading semiconductor technology and products, packaging solutions and engineering technology services to Original Equipment Manufacturer (OEM) clients.[2]
- *Software* consists primarily of operating systems and middleware. Included are DB2 information management software, Lotus software, Tivoli software, and WebSphere software, as well as integrated

tools designed to improve an organization's software development processes and capabilities.[2]

■ *Global Financing* is a business segment within IBM that is managed as if it were an independent entity. Its purpose is to facilitate the client's acquisition of IBM hardware, software, and services, and its mission is to generate a return on equity. It consists of three lines of business: (1) Customer financing, which provides lease and loan financing to end users and internal customers; (2) Commercial financing, which provides short-term inventory and accounts receivable financing to dealers; and (3) Remarketing, which sells or leases used equipment to customers.[3]

■ *Enterprise Investments* develops and provides industry-specific software and products. Its product life cycle management software helps IBM's industrial clients to manage the development and manufacturing of their products. Its document processing technologies serve the Financial Services sector and include products that enable electronic banking.[2]

■ *Personal Systems* develops and sells hardware, software, and services for customers and businesses of all sizes. It consists of three worldwide business units: the Personal Computing Division, the Printing Systems Division, and Retail Store Solutions.[6] In December 2004, it was announced that Lenovo Group Limited, the largest IT company in China, would acquire IBM's Personal Computing Division. The $1.75 billion transaction was finalized during the second quarter of 2005.[7]

In addition to the business segments described, there are three company-wide organizations that are instrumental to IBM's success: Sales and Distribution, Integrated Supply Chain, and Research and Development. The account representatives in the Sales and Distribution organization work in integrated teams to sell and deliver IBM products and services to clients. These teams include Global Services consultants, hardware and software brand specialists, online and telephone sales and assistance operators, independent software vendors, and resellers.[2] IBM spends approximately $41 billion annually through its Integrated Supply Chain, procuring materials and services around the world to support its supply, manufacturing and distribution processes.[2] IBM's Research and Development (R&D) operations distinguish it from its competitors. Since 1996, the company has invested between $5 and $6 billion annually for R&D, and the results of its investments are apparent. IBM received 3,248 U.S. patents in 2004. This marked the twelfth consecutive year that IBM was awarded more U.S. patents than any other company. Between 1993 and 2004, IBM was granted a total of 29,019 U.S. patents, more than its top ten competitors combined.[4]

In January 2005, IBM announced that it would pledge 500 of its software patents for open source use. IBM's intent is to help form an industry-wide "patent commons," in which patents are used to establish a platform for commercial innovation and software interoperability. The pledge applies to any individual, organization, or company working on or using software that meets the Open Source Initiative definition of open source software.[2] IBM's strength in R&D and its advocacy of open standards form the foundation of this case study.

IBM Watson Research—Global Security Analysis Lab

The Global Security Analysis Lab (GSAL) is part of IBM's Research and Development operations. GSAL was formed in 1995 for the purpose of advancing computer security expertise within IBM.[8] It consists of two teams. The larger of the teams is based at the Watson Research Center in Hawthorne, New York. The other GSAL team is based at the Zurich Research Lab in Switzerland. This case study deals with GSAL at the Watson Research Center.

The Watson GSAL works with several of the company's operational segments, among them Global Services, Systems and Technology, Software, and Personal Systems.[9] When the team was first formed, their focus was on offensive hacking and they became known as IBM's "ethical hackers."[8] Their efforts now are geared more toward testing and defending against network threats that exploit system vulnerabilities. (Appendix A summarizes these network threats.) Described next are the results of the Watson GSAL's collaborative efforts and groundbreaking research in the application of hardware support to enable trust.

Embedded Security Subsystem Version 1.0

When the Watson GSAL and the Personal Systems business segment began working together on a hardware-based means of user authentication, they initially considered the use of smart cards and readers. This option was determined to be too costly and too inflexible, so the team developed a smaller, cheaper, and more adaptable solution in the form of a trusted computing chip.[9] Known as the Embedded Security Subsystem (ESS), the chip provided a stronger method of user authentication.

ESS Version 1.0 (ESS 1.0) was an integrated circuit chip mounted on a daughtercard of an IBM desktop computer or on the motherboard of an IBM notebook computer. The chip interfaced with the System Management Bus (SMBus). The chip used the RSA algorithm to compute digital signatures using internally stored 512-bit or 1024-bit keys.[10] (The RSA algorithm is summarized in Appendix B.) The chip also used the private RSA keys to decrypt relatively small blocks of data, such as symmetric (secret) cryptographic keys that were necessary for file decryption operations. The private RSA keys were stored in registers inside the chip. These keys could be configured to remain inside the hardware, allowing the chip to protect their confidentiality and integrity and to prevent their unauthorized use.[10]

The digital signature and decryption operations were based on two types of RSA key pairs: hardware and user-specified. The hardware key pair was stored on the chip during its initialization. An administrator could use the hardware key pair to generate a digital signature, or a user could use the hardware key pair to decrypt other keys that were stored in the system, outside of the ESS chip. The user-specified key pairs could be generated, encrypted with the hardware public key, and stored in the system in which the chip was embedded. To generate a digital signature, the user's private RSA key was decrypted by the chip and stored in an internal chip register. Any data within the chip (e.g., the decrypted keys) were not accessible by other system components.[10]

Access to the chip's functions required the use of a password. A *hardware password*, which was stored in a register in the chip, was required for all administrative and configuration actions (e.g., changing the hardware public/private key pair). A *failure counter reset password*, also stored in a register in the chip, was associated with the chip's authentication failure handling mechanism to protect against password cracking attacks. After a specified number of failed password attempts, the chip locked users out for progressively longer periods of time.[10] This password was required to reset the counter for password failures. The user password was optional. At the user's discretion, a password could be specified to control access to the user's decrypted private RSA key when it was stored in a buffer within the chip.[10]

At the time of its development, ESS 1.0 was not based on open standards. IBM began to offer its proprietary chip in its PL300 desktops and T23 ThinkPad notebooks in 1999. In October 2001, the company received a Common Criteria EAL3 rating for its IBM Cryptographic Security Chip for PC Clients, which was used in ESS 1.0. (The Common Criteria is described in Appendix C.)

In 2002, IBM shifted its strategy to an on-demand operating environment, in which it focused on computing and network infrastructure that was based on industry-wide (open) standards rather than proprietary technologies. Successful open source operating systems (e.g., Linux) and programming languages (e.g., Java) had emerged, and IBM was aware that other companies were working on hardware-based methods of user authentication that were similar to its ESS chip. In IBM's view, the trusted authentication problem required an open source solution; an investment in this technology offered potentially greater returns than those it could earn by retaining proprietary control. IBM was able to build on its leadership in the Trusted Computing Platform Alliance (TCPA), and later in the Trusted Computing Group, to develop an ESS based on industry standards.

Promoting Open Standards

The TCPA was established in 1999 by IBM, Microsoft Corporation, Intel Corporation, Compaq, and Hewlett-Packard. The purpose of the alliance was to develop industry-wide standards for a trusted computing subsystem for microcomputers.[11] IBM's ESS 1.0 chip, which had already been developed, served as the prototype. Additional functionality was incorporated into the chip, and the Trusted Platform Module (described in the next section) became the central part of the TCPA specification.

In 2003, the TCPA became the Trusted Computing Group (TCG). The new group was created to develop and promote industry-wide standards for hardware-enabled trusted computing. Approximately ninety-five companies are members of the TCG,[12] and the group is led by seven promoter organizations: IBM, Microsoft Corporation, Intel Corporation, Hewlett-Packard, AMD, Sony Corporation, and Sun Microsystems, Inc. When the TCG was formed, it adopted the TCPA specifications, and it has since enhanced and extended these specifications across multiple platforms.

Embedded Security Subsystem Version 2.0

ESS 2.0 is based on the Trusted Platform Module: a TCG specification for a special-purpose integrated circuit chip that stores cryptographic keys, digital certificates, and passwords. The ESS 2.0 chip can generate public/private key pairs using the RSA algorithm. It also can compute digital signatures and encrypt/decrypt small blocks of data. The chip's cryptographic functions, trusted boot functions, and initialization and management functions are activated and enabled through the basic input/output system (BIOS).[13]

There are three types of cryptographic keys stored in the chip's nonvolatile memory: the endorsement key, the storage root key, and the owner authorization secret key (Table 4-1). The *endorsement key* is etched into the chip at the time of manufacture. It consists of a 2048-bit RSA public/private key pair that is never transmitted outside of the chip. The private RSA key is used to generate the chip's digital signature. This forms a unique identity for the chip that can be used to validate the device on the network. The digital signature is created using the RSA algorithm and either the SHA-1 or the SHA-256 secure hash algorithm (see Appendix D). The public portion of the RSA key is used to encrypt sensitive data that is sent to the chip, such as the system owner's password that is used to create the storage root key.[13]

The *storage root key* is created by the system owner. Comparable to Administrator in Windows operating systems or Root in UNIX and Linux operating systems, the owner must supply a password that is used to create

TABLE 4-1 An Overview of the ESS 2.0 Chip

CRYPTOGRAPHIC CAPABILITIES	NONVOLATILE MEMORY	VOLATILE MEMORY
Secure hash unit	Endorsement key	Platform configuration registers
RSA key pair generation	Storage root key	
RSA digital signature creation	Owner authorization secret key	RSA key temporary storage areas
RSA encryption/ decryption		

Source: David Safford, Ph.D., Manager, Global Security Analysis Lab, IBM Watson Research Center, May 5, 2005.

the storage root key. The key consists of a 2048-bit RSA public/private key pair. The public portion is used to encrypt other keys so that they can be stored on disk or in system memory, external to the chip. The private portion is used to decrypt these keys so that they can be used for other purposes, such as accessing encrypted files. The private portion of the storage root key never leaves the chip's nonvolatile memory.[13]

The *owner authorization secret key* is created by the system owner. This key consists of a 160-bit hash value of the owner's password. The value, which remains stored in the chip's nonvolatile memory, is used to authorize certain owner-related commands, such as the encryption or decryption of other cryptographic keys.[13]

Up to ten RSA public/private key pairs can be generated by the chip and stored in the chip's volatile memory (see Table 4-1). The RSA key pairs can be used either for digital signatures or for encryption/decryption operations. The public portion of each RSA key pair can be stored outside of the chip. However, the chip offers different treatment for the private portion of the RSA key pairs. The private RSA keys used to create digital signatures are stored in registers inside of the chip. They are never exported outside of the chip. In contrast, the private RSA keys used for decryption operations can be stored outside the chip. Before they are exported, the private RSA keys are encrypted inside the chip using the owner authorization secret key and the public portion of the storage root key. When the private RSA keys are needed, they are loaded into the chip's volatile memory and they are decrypted using the owner authorization secret key and the private portion of the storage root key.[13]

In addition to the cryptographic functions described, the ESS 2.0 chip provides trusted boot functions to help ensure the integrity of the system's platform. This is done by measuring, storing, and comparing system characteristics as the system boots up.

When the system is initially configured, the chip measures the BIOS, the master boot record (MBR), and other designated files associated with the system's configuration as the system boots up. The chip uses a secure hash algorithm (usually SHA-1) to internally calculate 160-bit hash values of these measurements. The hash values are encrypted within the chip using the public portion of the storage root key. The encrypted hash values, which represent the original state of the system, are stored outside of the chip, typically on the hard disk.[14]

Each time that the system is rebooted, it performs a self-check. The chip measures the same system configuration files as the system boots up. The chip uses the same secure hash algorithm to internally calculate 160-bit hash values of the current measurements. These hash values are stored in Platform Configuration Registers (PCRs) located inside of the chip, in the chip's volatile memory.[14]

A comparison of the platform measurements occurs next. The encrypted hash values, representing the system's initial state, are retrieved from external storage and decrypted inside of the chip using the private portion of the storage root key. The decrypted hash values are compared with the hash values that represent the system's current state, which are stored in the PCRs.[14] If the hash values match, the system continues to boot up. Hash values that do not match indicate that the system has been changed (e.g., infected by malicious code). At this point, either the boot process can be stopped or an integrity report can be generated.[15]

In addition to ensuring the integrity of the system's platform, the trusted boot functions help to protect the private RSA keys that are used for digital signing and for decryption operations. As discussed, these private keys are part of the RSA key pairs that are generated by the chip. The RSA key pairs typically are associated with the system characteristics that existed during boot up. The keys can be used only when the hash values of the current system measurements match the hash values that existed when the RSA key pairs were created.[14]

The chip's ability to protect the externally stored private RSA keys ultimately helps to protect the security of sensitive user files. User files typically are encrypted using a symmetric cryptosystem, such as the Data Encryption Standard (DES), Triple DES (3DES), or the Advanced Encryption

Standard (AES). The confidentiality and integrity of the user's files depend on the secrecy of the symmetric key used to encrypt and decrypt the files. The public portion of the RSA key pair can be used to encrypt the symmetric key that was used to encrypt the user files. The corresponding private portion of the RSA key pair is used to decrypt the symmetric key, which is needed to decrypt the user files. During the trusted boot process, if the hash values of the current system measurements do not match the hash values of the initial system configuration, the private RSA keys will not be decrypted. As a result, the underlying symmetric keys will not be decrypted, and the user files will not be accessible.

Software is being written to extend the process of measuring, storing, and comparing system characteristics beyond the boot process to the more dynamic runtime environment of system operation.[16] Applications are being developed to ensure that only correctly configured systems can access the network and to verify the integrity of application software.

Controlling the ESS 2.0 Chip

All of the chip's functions are controlled through the BIOS. Before the ESS 2.0 chip can be used, its functions must be initiated by the system owner through a BIOS setup utility. The BIOS activates the chip and enables the chip's functions through a start-up command. This command allows the system owner to do one of three things. The start-up command can allow the system owner to deactivate the chip until the next time the system is powered on. Optionally, the command can activate the chip with the hash values in the PCRs restored from a saved state, so that the system can resume operations from a suspended condition. More frequently though, the start-up command is used to initiate the chip with the PCRs cleared, so that the hash values of the current system configuration can be calculated and stored during the trusted boot process.[13]

The BIOS allows the system owner to enter the password necessary to create the storage root key and the owner authorization secret key.

The BIOS also allows the system owner to clear and reset these keys.[13] The chip's cryptographic functions, trusted boot functions, and initialization and management functions are hardware based. The chip's functionality is established through the BIOS, and the chip uses its own firmware and circuits for processing operations.

Final Comments

Trusted hardware is the foundation for trusted systems. IBM's ESS 2.0 chip provides stronger user authentication, device validation, and system integrity, and therefore greater system trust. ESS 2.0 is based on open standards for an integrated circuit chip that stores cryptographic keys, digital certificates, and passwords. Its functions are self-contained and its registers provide trusted storage. Because the chip does not depend on any software for its operations, the contents of the chip are better protected against software vulnerabilities, software-based attacks, and unauthorized access. The contents of the chip also are protected from theft; any attempt to remove the chip from the daughtercard or the motherboard causes it to disable itself, so that the data stored inside of the chip becomes inaccessible.

ESS 2.0 is available on certain IBM NetVista desktops and ThinkPad notebooks. The chip works with IBM Client Security Software, a downloadable software component that supports additional access control devices (e.g., fingerprint readers) and provides an interface to other application software.

Appendix A

Network Threats

Passwords are the most frequently used, and the weakest, means of user authentication. The use of poorly chosen, widely known, openly displayed, or publicly disclosed passwords virtually guarantees unauthorized access to user- and administrative-level accounts. The use of strong passwords can be undermined if a keystroke logger has been installed on the system, or if the passwords are stored or transmitted in unencrypted form. Several programs transmit passwords in plaintext, among them telnet, ftp, HTTP, and the Berkeley r-services of commands (e.g., rlogin).

Network shares (e.g., NetBIOS) that are not configured properly could expose critical system files or provide a mechanism for an attacker to take control. These problems can occur when users attempt to make their drives readable and writeable by other known parties (e.g., co-workers), but improperly configure their network shares to allow open access to all.

Hypertext transfer protocol (HTTP) servers, such as Apache or Microsoft's Internet Information Server (IIS), are vulnerable to attack. If their service packs and security updates are not current or if the servers have been configured improperly, they are susceptible to malicious code (e.g., viruses, worms, Trojan horses), denial of service (DoS), and directory traversal attacks. Sensitive data could be disclosed or unwanted code could be executed. Root access also could be attained by an attacker, resulting in a total compromise of the server.

Certain operating system processes are susceptible to buffer overflow attacks. Buffer overflows are the result of careless code development and poor programming practices. The overflow condition occurs when an input string exceeds the size of the buffer (a fixed array in memory). The excess data may be placed on the process stack, corrupting whatever data were there previously. The overflow can be exploited by an attacker to execute malicious code, allowing the attacker to gain control of the machine.

Network file system (NFS) is a frequent target of attack in UNIX networks. NFS treats remote files and directories as if they were stored locally. If the server is incorrectly configured, file systems can be exported with improper permissions, allowing attackers easy access.

Network information service (NIS) is another frequent target of attack in UNIX networks. NIS client tools can be used to guess the domain name of server; a particularly easy feat for an attacker if an obvious string (e.g., the company's name) is used. Once the domain name is known, an attacker can use a remote procedure call (RPC) query to access the mappings of each host's critical information, including the contents of the passwd file. Other attacks, such as phishing, pharming, spamming, the use of botnets, and directory harvest attacks can increase the server load, resulting in a DoS.

Additional information about current network threats and critical Internet security vulnerabilities can be located at the SANS (SysAdmin, Audit, Network, Security) Institute site: http://www.sans.org/top20/.

Appendix B

RSA Algorithm

The RSA algorithm is an asymmetric (public key) cryptosystem that was invented by Ronald Rivest, Adi Shamir, and Leonard Adleman in 1977. In an asymmetric cryptosystem, a user has two keys: a public key and a private key. The public key can be openly shared, but the private key must be accessible only to its owner. Both keys are derived from two randomly generated, large prime numbers. Although the private key is mathematically related to the public key, deriving the private key from the public key requires factoring. Security is based on the computational infeasibility of factoring very large numbers.

The RSA algorithm can be used for encryption and decryption operations. The sender can use the receiver's public key to encrypt the message, and the receiver can use his private key to decrypt the message. However, because asymmetric cryptosystems tend to be slow, use of the RSA algorithm for encryption and decryption operations usually is restricted to protecting other cryptographic keys. Sensitive user files typically are encrypted using a symmetric cryptosystem, such as DES, 3DES, or AES. These cryptosystems are computationally faster than the RSA algorithm. The drawback to symmetric cryptosystems is that the same key is used for both encryption and decryption operations. The confidentiality and integrity of the user's files depend on the secrecy of the symmetric key used to encrypt and decrypt the files. To protect the symmetric key from unauthorized disclosure during transmission, the sender can use the receiver's public RSA key to encrypt the symmetric key. The receiver can use his private RSA key to decrypt the symmetric key.

The RSA algorithm also can be used to generate and verify digital signatures. To generate a digital signature, the sender uses her private key to encrypt the message digest. A *message digest* is a condensed representation of the message that acts like a digital fingerprint of that message. Message digests are produced by hash algorithms, such as SHA-1 or SHA-256 (described in Appendix D). The sender's digital signature, which was formed by encrypting the message digest with the sender's private key, is attached to the message. Verifying the digital signature is a multistep process. The receiver uses the sender's public key to decrypt the sender's digital signature. This provides the receiver with the message digest that was used by the sender to create the digital signature. Next, the receiver must create the message digest by applying the same hash algorithm to the message. If the message digest that resulted from decrypting the sender's digital signature matches the message digest that was produced by the hash algorithm, the signature is verified as being genuine.

Because of the mathematics involved in the RSA algorithm, it is faster to encrypt data and to verify a digital signature than it is to decrypt data and to generate a digital signature.

There are many good books and websites that discuss cryptography and its applications. Examples include Bruce Schneier's book, *Applied Cryptography* (John Wiley & Sons, Inc., 1996) and the RSA Laboratories website, Crypto FAQ Section Index, http://www.rsasecurity.com/rsalabs/node.asp?id=2153.

Appendix C

Common Criteria

The Common Criteria became an international standard in 1999. Also known as ISO/IEC (International Organization for Standardization/ International Electrotechnical Commission) 15408, it supports the specification and evaluation of security features in products and systems.

A number of organizations were involved in the development of the Common Criteria: the Communications Security Establishment in Canada, the Direction Centrale de la Sécurité des Systèmes d'Informations in France, the Bundesamt für Sicherheit in der Informationstechnik in Germany, the Netherlands National Communications Security Agency in the Netherlands, the Communications-Electronics Security Group in the United Kingdom, and the National Institute of Standards and Technology (NIST) and the National Security Agency (NSA) in the United States.

Common Criteria certification in the United States is awarded by the National Information Assurance Partnership (NIAP), a collaborative association between NIST and NSA. The certification process begins when a vendor submits its information technology product or system (referred to as the Target of Evaluation) and a description of its security functions, assurance measures and assertions (referred to as the Security Target) to a Common Criteria Testing Laboratory. There are nine such laboratories in the United States, and all are approved by NIAP as commercial IT security testing laboratories: Arca Common Criteria Testing Laboratory (Sterling, VA), Booz Allen Hamilton Common Criteria Testing Laboratory (Linthicum, MD), COACT Inc. CAFE Laboratory (Columbia, MD), Computer Sciences Corporation (Annapolis Junction, MD), Criterian Independent Labs (Fairmont, WV), CygnaCom Solutions' Security Evaluation Laboratory (McLean, VA), InfoGard Laboratories, Inc. (San Luis Obispo, CA), Lockheed Martin IS&S SSO (Hanover, MD), and SAIC Common Criteria Testing Laboratory (Columbia, MD). The vendor must pay a fee to the laboratory for the security evaluation to be performed.

Depending on the outcome of the security evaluation, the Target of Evaluation may be awarded an Evaluation Assurance Level (EAL) rating. The assurance levels range from low to high and are defined in EAL ratings that are hierarchically numbered. Targets of Evaluation may be certified at EAL1 (functionally tested), EAL2 (structurally tested), EAL3 (methodically tested and checked), EAL4 (methodically designed, tested, and reviewed), EAL5 (semiformally designed and tested), EAL6 (semiformally verified design and tested), and EAL7 (formally verified design and tested).

Commercial products or systems typically are certified at EAL1 through EAL4. At these lower level ratings, additional controls can be retrofitted to products or systems that have already been developed. Products or systems that are certified at EAL5 through EAL7 must have been designed and developed with the intent of achieving a higher level EAL rating. These products or systems require the use of progressively specialized security engineering methods in increasingly rigorous development environments. Typically used for defense-related purposes, these targets of evaluation are intended for high-risk environments where the value of the assets to be protected can offset the substantial cost of product or system development.

The Common Criteria is described in detail in NIST Special Publication 800-23, "Guide to Federal Organizations on Security Assurance and Acquisition/Use of Tested/Evaluated Products," August 2000, available at http://csrc.nist.gov/publications/nistpubs/800-23/sp800-23.pdf.

Appendix D

SHA-1 and SHA-256

A secure hash algorithm (SHA) takes a variable-length message and produces a fixed-length value for that message called a *message digest*. A hash algorithm is determined to be secure if it is one way and collision free. *One way* means that it is computationally infeasible to find a message that corresponds to a given message digest. *Collision free* means that it is computationally infeasible to find two different messages that produce the same message digest.

SHA-1 takes a variable-length message that is no longer than 2^{64} bits and produces a 160-bit message digest. It is designed so that the likelihood of finding a collision is 1 in 2^{80}. In February 2005, three Chinese cryptographers announced that they had developed an algorithm that was able to find collisions faster than using a brute force attack. Using their algorithm, the likelihood of finding a collision is 1 in 2^{69}.

SHA-256 is a stronger variation of SHA-1. SHA-256 takes a variable-length message that is no longer than 2^{64} bits and produces a 256-bit message digest. It is designed so that the likelihood of finding a collision is 1 in 2^{128}.

SHA-1 and SHA-256 are described in Federal Information Processing Standards Publication 180-2, "Announcing the Secure Hash Standard," August 1, 2002, available at http://csrc.nist.gov/publications/fips/fips180-2/fips180-2withchangenotice.pdf.

Endnotes

1. "History of IBM, 1910s." Available: http://www-03.ibm.com/ibm/history/history/decade_1910.html.
2. U.S. Securities and Exchange Commission, Form 10-K, "Annual Report for the Year Ended December 31, 2004, International Business Machines Corporation." Available: http://www.sec.gov/Archives/edgar/data/51143/000104746905004595/a2152314z10-k.htm.
3. U.S. Securities and Exchange Commission, Form 10-K, Exhibit 13, "Financial Report." Available: http://www.sec.gov/Archives/edgar/data/51143/000104746905004595/a2152314zex-13.htm.
4. "Understanding Our Company, an IBM Prospectus." Available: ftp://ftp.software.ibm.com/annualreport/2004/2004_ibm_prospectus.pdf.
5. Each of the six operational segments, and their business, infrastructure and component value capabilities, are described in Part I of IBM's 2004 SEC Filings, Form 10-K. See Endnote 2.
6. Check Point Software Technologies Ltd., "OPSEC Partners." Available: http://www.opsec.com/solutions/partners/ibm_ess.html.

7. Lemon, S., "Lenovo Completes Acquisition of IBM's PC Unit," *Computerworld,* May 2, 2005. Available: http://www.computerworld.com/news/2005/story/0,11280,101490,00.html.

8. "IBM Research—Global Security Analysis Lab." Available: http://www.research.ibm.com/gsal.

9. Personal communication with David Safford, Ph.D., Manager, Global Security Analysis Lab, IBM Watson Research Center, March 21, 2005.

10. National Institute of Standards and Technology and National Security Agency, "Common Criteria Evaluation and Validation Scheme Validation Report, IBM Cryptographic Security Chip for PC Clients Manufactured by ATMEL, Report Number CCEVS-VR-01-0005, October 10, 2001." Available: http://www.commoncriteriaportal.org/public/files/epfiles/CCEVS-VID300-VR-01-0005.pdf.

11. Safford, D., "The Need for TCPA," October 2002. Available: http://www.research.ibm.com/gsal/tcpa/why_tcpa.pdf.

12. A list of the TCG member organizations can be found at https://www.trustedcomputinggroup.org/about/members/.

13. Safford, D., "Take Control of TCPA," July 31, 2003. Available: http://www.linuxjournal.com/article/6633.

14. Personal communication with David Safford, Ph.D., Manager, Global Security Analysis Lab, IBM Watson Research Center, May 5, 2005.

15. Personal communication with David Safford, Ph.D., Manager, Global Security Analysis Lab, IBM Watson Research Center, April 29, 2005.

16. Sailer, R., van Doorn, L., and Ward, J. P., "IBM Research Report: The Role of TPM in Enterprise Security," October 6, 2004. Available: https://www.trustedcomputinggroup.org/press/news_articles/rc23363.pdf.

CASE STUDY QUESTIONS

1. Why is it essential to have a hardware security foundation?
2. Identify at least five attacks that cannot be defended with software.

3. Why are open standards important in security?

4. Why would IBM be an advocate for open standards? Why would it change its proprietary ESS 1.0 chip—which it had already sold in some of its PL300 desktops and T23 ThinkPad notebooks, and which it had paid a Common Criteria Testing Laboratory to evaluate—so that it was available as open source?

5. What does *trusted computing* mean?

6. What is the trusted platform module?

7. Describe the major differences between ESS 1.0 and ESS 2.0.

8. How can the trusted boot functions prevent the unauthorized modification of the operating system?

9. What is the purpose of the endorsement key? The storage root key? The owner authorization secret key?

10. Explain how the ESS 2.0 chip can protect the owner's data from external attack, but it cannot protect that data from attack by the owner.

KEY TERMS

Advanced Encryption Standard (AES): Symmetric cryptosystem developed by Dr. Vincent Rijmen and Dr. Joan Daemen, originally named *Rijndael*. AES encrypts a 128-bit block of plaintext using a 128-, 192-, or 256-bit key to produce a 128-bit block of ciphertext. It was adopted as a Federal Information Processing Standard (FIPS) in November 2001, and is described in FIPS Publication 197, "Advanced Encryption Standard," available at http://csrc.nist.gov/publications/fips/fips197/fips-197.pdf. AES replaced the DES in May 2002.

Asymmetric Cryptosystem: Public key cryptosystem in which the encryption and decryption operations use two different, but mathematically related, keys.

Authentication: Process that verifies a user's or a system's identity.

Bandwidth: Frequency range of a communication line. Determines how much data can be transmitted in a given amount of time.

Basic Input/Output System (BIOS): It is stored on a read only memory chip on the computer's motherboard, and it contains the basic instructions needed to initialize the hardware and boot the computer.

Berkeley r-services: Collection of client/server applications used in the Berkeley Software Distribution version of UNIX. Examples include remote login (rlogin) and remote execution of commands (rexec). These programs often create security problems.

Botnet: Network of compromised machines that are controlled by software robots. Machines can be controlled remotely and be used to perpetuate other types of attack, such as DoS attacks, viruses, Trojan horses, spam, and directory harvest attacks.

Brute Force Attack: Method of defeating a cryptosystem by exhausting all possibilities until the solution is found.

Buffer Overflow: Condition that occurs when an input string is larger than the size of the computer's memory that is used to store data. Excess data may be placed on the process stack, overwriting whatever data were there previously. The computer can execute whatever malicious code is contained in the overflow.

Ciphertext: Unreadable message produced from an encryption process.

Confidentiality: Preventing the unauthorized disclosure of data or information.

Cryptosystem: Short for cryptographic system. Includes the algorithm, protocols, procedures, and instructions needed to encrypt and decrypt messages.

Data Encryption Standard (DES): Symmetric cryptosystem that encrypts a 64-bit block of plaintext using an effective key size of 56 bits to produce a 64-bit block of ciphertext. It was adopted as a Federal Information Processing Standard in November 1976. It was revised in 1993 and is described in FIPS Publication 46-2, "Data Encryption Standard (DES)," available at http://www.itl.nist.gov/fipspubs/fip46-2.htm. In May 2002, DES was replaced by AES.

Daughtercard: Circuit board that plugs into the motherboard. It can directly access memory and the central processing unit.

Denial of Service (DoS): Loss of network or computer services by users. It is typically caused by an attack that depletes network bandwidth or overburdens a system's resources.

Digital Signature: Used to authenticate a device or a user. Created through the use of a message digest and the user's private key.

Directory Harvest Attack: Used to find legitimate e-mail addresses from mail servers. E-mail addresses of nonreturned spam are added to a database for further spamming.

Directory Traversal Attack: Used to take advantage of a particular software flaw to gain unauthorized access to restricted files that reside outside of the Web server's root directory.

Domain Name System (DNS) Server: System that associates domain (Internet) names with their corresponding IP addresses.

File Transfer Protocol (ftp): Internet software standard used to exchange files between remote computer systems.

Hash Algorithm: Mathematical function that takes a variable-length message and produces a fixed-length value for that message (message digest).

HyperText Transfer Protocol (HTTP): Most frequently used communication protocol on the World Wide Web. Used to exchange Web pages between servers and browsers.

Integrity: Preventing the unauthorized modification or destruction of information.

Keystroke Logger: A hardware device or a program used to capture user keystrokes.

Malicious Code: Software developed for the purpose of doing harm. Also known as *malicious software* or *malware.*

Master Boot Record (MBR): The first sector of a hard disk that contains the commands necessary to boot the system.

Message: Generic term for electronic data.

Message Digest: Condensed representation of a message that acts like a digital fingerprint of that message. Message digests are produced by hash algorithms.

Middleware: Software that acts as an intermediary between different applications.

Motherboard: Main circuit board. Contains the Central Processing Unit (CPU), memory, Basic Input/Output System (BIOS), serial and parallel ports, mass storage interfaces, expansion slots, controllers for peripheral devices, and connectors for attaching additional boards.

Multidimensional Organizational Structure: Also known as a *matrix organizational structure.* Simultaneously incorporates many different types of organizational structures (e.g., hierarchical structure, project structure, team structure, virtual structure).

Network File System (NFS): Protocol developed by Sun Microsystems, Inc., that treats remote files and directories as if they were stored locally. A primary networking component of UNIX systems.

Network Information Service (NIS): Protocol developed by Sun Microsystems, Inc., that acts as a directory service for network hosts. Formerly known as *Yellow Pages,* it is a primary networking component of UNIX systems.

Original Equipment Manufacturer (OEM): Company that manufactures computer equipment, which is sold to another vendor, who sells it to consumers.

Open Source Software: Software that can be freely used, modified, and redistributed.

Open Standards: Publicly available specifications that are vendor neutral and platform independent.

Operating System: Collection of programs that manages the basic functions and resources of a computer.

Passwd File: Administrative password file used in UNIX or Linux systems that contains user account records, including username and password information.

Pharming: Exploiting a domain name system (DNS) server software vulnerability so that traffic to a legitimate site is redirected to a fraudulent site. At the fraudulent site, users can be tricked into disclosing confidential personal information.

Phishing: Use of an apparently legitimate e-mail message to trick a user into disclosing confidential personal information.

Plaintext: Readable message, also known as *cleartext*.

Platform Configuration Register (PCR): Storage area in the chip's volatile memory. There are 16 PCRs in the ESS 2.0 chip. They store the hash values of the system's initialization and configuration information.

Register: High-speed storage area.

Remote Procedure Call (RPC): Protocol that allows a computer process to transparently communicate with a computer program running on a remote computer.

Spam: Unsolicited e-mail.

Spamming: Transmitting unsolicited e-mail.

Symmetric Cryptosystem: Secret key cryptosystem in which the encryption and decryption operations are based on the same key.

System Management Bus (SMBus): A two-wire bus used for low bandwidth system management communications, such as communicating with the ESS chip or the chip in a laptop's rechargeable battery pack.

telnet: Terminal emulation program used for logging in to a remote computer.

Triple DES (3DES): Symmetric cryptosystem that performs a DES encryption operation, followed by a DES decryption operation, followed by another DES encryption operation. It encrypts a 64-bit block of plaintext using an effective key size of 112 bits to produce a 64-bit block of ciphertext. It was adopted as a Federal Information Processing Standard in 1998, and is described in FIPS Publication 46-3, "Data Encryption Standard," available at http://csrc.nist.gov/publications/fips/fips46-3/fips46-3.pdf.

Trojan Horse: Apparently useful program that contains and conceals harmful or unwanted code.

Trusted Computing Platform Alliance (TCPA): Organization established in 1999 by IBM, Microsoft Corporation, Intel Corporation, Compaq, and Hewlett Packard to develop industry-wide standards for a trusted computing subsystem for microcomputers. The TCPA was the precursor to the Trusted Computing Group.

Trusted Computing Group (TCG): Organizational alliance established in 2003 to develop and promote industry-wide standards for hardware-enabled trusted computing. It evolved from the Trusted Computing Platform Alliance.

Trusted Platform Module: Special-purpose integrated circuit chip that provides fundamental security functions. These functions include the secure storage of keys used for digital signature and decryption operations, and a trusted boot process to help ensure the integrity of the system's platform. Specifications for the trusted platform module were established by the Trusted Computing Group.

Virus: Self-replicating, malicious piece of code.

Worm: Self-contained, self-replicating computer program that usually performs unwanted actions.

SRA International, Inc.:
Automating Compliance With Federal Information Security Requirements

F or federal agencies, verifying compliance with government information security regulations is a time-consuming and complicated task. Recent legislation requires each federal agency to conduct an annual evaluation of its information security program, which includes performing a separate risk assessment for each system and information asset, testing all information security policies and procedures, evaluating existing risks, developing remedial action plans, and preparing detailed reports. The complexity of the task is exacerbated by limitations in agency funding, potential misinterpretations of statutory requirements, and the large numbers of systems that comprise the information technology (IT) infrastructure of each federal agency.

This case study describes how SRA International, Inc., has automated the compliance process for federal government agencies through the use of its Web-based risk assessment software.

To provide necessary background information, the case study presents an overview of SRA International, Inc., outlines key aspects of the Federal Information Security Management Act, and summarizes relevant documents issued by the National Institute of Standards and Technology.

SRA International, Inc.—The Company

SRA International, Inc., is a leading provider of IT services and solutions to federal government clients. Currently, SRA provides IT support to thirteen of the fifteen federal departments in the executive branch, to all branches of the military services, and to the judicial and legislative branches of the federal government.[1]

SRA was incorporated in 1976 as Systems Research and Applications Corporation, and it began operations two years later. In 1984, a parent company was formed and incorporated as SRA International, Inc. It has been a publicly held company since May 24, 2002. Its class A common stock trades on the New York Stock Exchange under the symbol SRX.

SRA's corporate headquarters is located in Fairfax, Virginia. It operates forty-two offices in fifteen states and the District of Columbia, as well as one office in Canada. To more efficiently serve its federal government client base, SRA has located the greatest concentration of its offices (fifteen) in the Washington, D.C., metropolitan area. As of June 30, 2005, SRA employed 4,177 people. More than half have federal government security clearances, and approximately 96% are professionals in IT or related disciplines.[1]

The company's 2005 reported net income was $57,723,000 on total revenue of $881,770,000. Federal government clients accounted for ninety-nine percent of the company's revenue: sixty percent was derived from national security clients, twenty-nine percent from civilian agencies and departments, and ten percent from health care and public health clients. The remaining one percent of the company's revenue was attributable to its commercial clients.[1] As of June 30, 2005, SRA's backlog (orders for services under existing signed contracts) was approximately $2.7 billion.

Market Sectors

SRA provides IT services and solutions in three primary markets: national security, civil government, and health care and public health. A representative list of SRA's clients in each of these markets is shown in Tables 5-1, 5-2, and 5-3. SRA's largest market is national security. Within this market, SRA is a significant contributor to the C4ISR (command and control, communications, computers, intelligence, surveillance, and reconnaissance) systems that support the U.S. Department of Defense (DoD) and the U.S. Department of Homeland Security (DHS). SRA provides systems integration, program management, intelligence, surveillance, reconnaissance, and other technical services to support the mission-critical information systems and applications within DoD and DHS. In conjunction with DHS' Information Analysis and Infrastructure Protection Directorate, SRA supports and develops the plans, programs, and operations needed to protect the nation's physical and cyber infrastructures from attack or disruption. SRA also assists the Defense Advanced Research Projects Agency's Tactical Technology Office in evaluating technologies developed by industry, universities, and military laboratories.[1]

Also within the national security market, SRA supports the DoD information systems used by the Office of the Secretary of Defense, the defense agencies, the Joint Chiefs of Staff organizations, the three military departments (Army, Air Force, Navy), the four military services (Army, Air Force, Navy, Marine Corps), the National Guard, and the command structure. SRA's responsibilities typically involve the design, development, integration, and implementation of large, complex information systems. SRA also provides IT support to the Army Reserve Component. SRA manages and maintains the Reserve Component Automation System, which links more than 10,500 Army National Guard and U.S. Army Reserve units at approximately 4,000 sites worldwide. In addition, SRA has installed and upgraded more than 100 distance learning classrooms in support of the Army National Guard's Distributive Training Technology

TABLE 5-1 National Security—Representative Clients

Department of Defense
   Air Mobility Command
   Army National Guard
   Defense Advanced Research Projects Agency
   Defense Information Systems Agency
   Defense Logistics Agency
   Defense Manpower Data Center
   Department of the Air Force
   Department of the Army
   Department of the Navy
   Joint Chiefs of Staff
   Military Sealift Command
   Military Traffic Management Command
   Office of the Secretary of Defense
   U.S. Army Reserves
   U.S. Marine Corps
   U.S. Transportation Command
Department of Homeland Security
Various Intelligence Agencies

Source: SRA International, Inc., "Services & Solutions, Representative Clients."
Available: http://www.sra.com/services/index.asp?id=59.

TABLE 5-2 Civil Government—Representative Clients

Administrative Office of the U.S. Courts
Department of Agriculture
Department of Commerce
Department of the Interior
Department of Justice
Department of Labor
Department of Transportation
   Federal Aviation Administration

(continues)

TABLE 5-2 Civil Government—Representative Clients *(continued)*

Department of the Treasury
  Internal Revenue Service
Department of Veterans Affairs
Environmental Protection Agency
Federal Deposit Insurance Corporation
General Services Administration
Government Accountability Office
Library of Congress
National Aeronautics and Space Administration
National Archives and Records Administration
Pension Benefit Guaranty Corporation
Small Business Administration
U.S. Agency for International Development
U.S. Securities and Exchange Commission

Source: SRA International, Inc., "Services & Solutions, Representative Clients."
Available: http://www.sra.com/services/index.asp?id=59.

TABLE 5-3 Health Care and Public Health—Representative Clients

Department of Defense
  Army Medical Command
  Office of the Secretary of Defense (Health Affairs)
Department of Health and Human Services
  Administration for Children and Families
  Centers for Disease Control and Prevention
  Centers for Medicare & Medicaid Services
  Food and Drug Administration
  Health Resources & Services Administration
  National Institutes of Health
  Office of the Secretary

Source: SRA International, Inc., "Services & Solutions, Representative Clients."
Available: http://www.sra.com/services/index.asp?id=59.

Project.[1] The classrooms are connected by a nationwide Asynchronous Transfer Mode network that accommodates the simultaneous transfer of voice, video, and data.[2]

SRA has helped agencies in the civil government sector use technology to enhance their productivity, improve information sharing, and provide better service. For example, in fiscal year 2004, SRA designed a consolidated local area network for the Federal Aviation Administration, deployed two online self-service sites for the Pension Benefit Guaranty Corporation, provided development, support, and training for the Department of Veterans Affairs' Office of Cyber and Information Security intranet portal, managed more than 150 servers and 4,000 desktop systems in a nationwide network that links the users and offices of the National Archives and Records Administration, and provided 24–7 on-site IT infrastructure support for more than 3,800 users from the Government Accountability Office (GAO) located at a dozen sites throughout the United States. In addition, SRA has upgraded and continues to manage the IT program for the U.S. Agency for International Development, an independent federal agency that provides economic, development, and humanitarian assistance to nations throughout the world. Among the services provided by SRA are systems and network engineering, IT operations security, worldwide data and voice communications, software and application development, and customer relationship and technical management services.[3]

In the health care and public health sector, SRA's clients include military organizations within the DoD's Health Services System and civil organizations within the U.S. Department of Health and Human Services (DHHS). In 2004, SRA was awarded a ten-year Defense Systems Integration, Design, Development, Operations, and Maintenance Services contract. Under this contract, SRA is responsible for maintaining and enhancing the battlefield and domestic systems that store medical data for service members and their families.[3] SRA also has supported several IT initiatives for DHHS. It redesigned the DHHS website, and incorporated enterprise-wide search features and an e-mail response system to improve DHHS' service to citizens. It also helped to implement the first department-wide use of public key infrastructure within DHHS, which established trusted government-to-government and government-to-business transactions between DHHS employees and contractors. In addition, SRA designed, engineered, and continues to operate the nation-wide web-based systems of the National Practitioner Data Bank and the Healthcare Integrity and Protection Data Bank. These systems maintain data and produce reports on adverse actions taken against health care practitioners, providers, and suppliers.[3]

Services and Business Solutions

SRA offers a range of services that spans the IT life cycle. The company categorizes these services into three groups. Its *strategic consulting* services include the formulation of business plans to address client IT needs, and the identification and implementation of technological changes to improve the client's performance, cost effectiveness, and quality of service. Its *systems design, development, and integration* services include project management, systems engineering, security engineering, network design, software development, enterprise application integration, database and data warehouse design and development, testing and evaluation, config-uration management, training, and implementation support. This ser-vice group is responsible for developing system concepts, defining requirements, designing architectures, and integrating complex mission-critical systems. Its *outsourcing and operations management* services are intended to help government clients reduce their costs of operations and respond to the declining federal government IT labor force. SRA accom-plishes these objectives by managing the client's technical infrastructures, operating and managing the client's networks, and in cases of extreme need, managing and operating the client's entire business processes.[1]

SRA also has developed a number of core business solutions that apply to SRA's clients in the national security, civil government, and health care and public health markets. These business solutions focus on common operational requirements, and are based on reusable tools, techniques, and methods.

- SRA's *text and data mining* operations can extract and analyze massive volumes of data to identify patterns of activity, trends, or correlations. SRA has developed NetOwl text mining software tools to collect, search, organize, and analyze unstructured text (e.g., newspapers, web pages, and reports) written in different languages, including English, Arabic, French, Chinese, Farsi, Korean, and Spanish.[1] Other software applications, such as SRA's ORIONMagic knowledge management software, can collect, extract, transform, analyze, and store data from structured sources (e.g., spreadsheets, databases, and data warehouses). SRA's text and data mining software have been used by several federal government agencies. For example, the Internal Revenue Service (IRS) uses a fraud detection system that SRA developed. The system uses advanced data mining techniques to construct models that are applied to electronic and paper tax returns to highlight potential patterns of refund fraud.[1]

- SRA's *contingency and disaster response planning* operations help government agencies prepare for, respond to, and recover from national security emergencies and natural disaster situations. SRA works with its federal government clients to assess site-specific threats, determine essential functions, and identify activities needed to sustain their operations. SRA has developed continuity of operations plans for major DoD organizations, including clients within the Departments of the Army, Navy, and Air Force, the Defense Information Systems Agency, and the Office of the Secretary of Defense. In addition, SRA has developed continuity of operations plans for civilian agencies, such as the Library of Congress and the U.S. Department of Agriculture (USDA) Forest Service.[1]

- SRA's *information assurance and critical infrastructure protection* operations help clients to detect, react, and respond to a variety of system threats, such as malicious code, hackers, espionage, and natural disasters. SRA's capabilities include security engineering, vulnerability analyses, regulatory compliance, penetration testing, intrusion detection and response systems, backup and recovery planning, incident response and forensic services, and security awareness training. Its clients include the DoD, DHS, DHHS, GAO, the U.S. Department of the Treasury, and the Environmental Protection Agency (EPA).[1]

- SRA's *environmental strategies* include management consulting, analytical services, policy analyses, and IT implementations.[1] In this area, SRA has worked most extensively with the EPA. SRA is a major support contractor for the EPA's Brownfields, Superfund, and ENERGY STAR programs.[4,5,6] It provides information management, Web services, regulatory and policy analysis, facilitation and training, and communication services to help the EPA's Office of Brownfields Cleanup and Redevelopment effectively manage its program. SRA also develops applications for the EPA's Superfund Web site, helps the EPA process documents for public access and dissemination, and conducts Superfund site data analyses. SRA also has developed an enterprise database that stores critical information for the EPA's Climate Protection Partnerships Division ENERGY STAR program. Information stored in the database is used to populate the ENERGY STAR public outreach Web sites. In addition, SRA has developed and implemented a portfolio manager application on the Web that assists ENERGY STAR participant companies in assessing the energy consumption of their commercial buildings.[3]

- SRA's *conflict management and dispute resolution* operations support collaborative decision making, case mediation and arbitration, situation assessment, conflict management, coaching and mentoring, training, research, and evaluation. For example, SRA has provided the EPA with software tools to help resolve a variety of disputes, ranging from community issues to national environmental policy conflicts.[1]

■ SRA uses *enterprise architecture* to help government clients unify their computer systems, networks, databases, and processes. Through the use of common hardware and software, federal agency systems can more easily communicate and share data. This improved interoperability is necessary for national security purposes. SRA has provided enterprise architecture support for the U.S. Department of Defense's Missile Defense Agency, the National Institutes of Health (NIH), the USDA, the IRS, the EPA and the GAO.[1]

■ SRA's *network operations and management* solutions include network design and migration, systems and database administration, proactive monitoring for network performance and availability, enterprise backup and recovery, and video and data network consolidation. SRA provides network engineering and operations services for several federal government agencies, including the Puget Sound Naval Shipyard, NIH, and the GAO. SRA also manages the enterprise operations center for GuardNet XXI, a nationwide telecommunications structure that serves as the communication channel for voice, video, and data between the Department of the Army and more than 30,000 Army National Guard users in the fifty states, the District of Columbia, and three U.S. territories.[3]

■ SRA's *enterprise systems management* solutions cover requirements definition, design and architecture development, systems and network management, workflow and configuration management, performance monitoring and reporting, software distribution and patch management, and data backup and recovery. SRA directed the IRS' agency-wide implementation of IBM's Tivoli enterprise systems management software, and it currently helps to provide online support to more than 110,000 users from the IRS. In addition to the IRS, SRA has provided enterprise systems management support to the U.S. Army, the Department of Veterans Affairs, the U.S. Department of Defense's Missile Defense Agency, the GAO, and the USDA Forest Service.[1]

■ SRA's *wireless integration* services include life-cycle consulting and security planning, enterprise deployment and integration, and application development. For example, SRA designed, developed, and implemented the deployment of more than 6,000 of Research In Motion's Blackberry devices within DHHS. This wireless deployment, one of the largest in the federal government, has improved DHHS' workflow by enabling real-time data collection, analysis, and decision making. SRA also uses radio frequency identification (RFID) technology as an automatic, wireless method of collecting product, place, time, or transaction data. SRA has integrated RFID technology to help the DoD track military personnel, equipment, and cargo throughout the world in real time.[1]

■ SRA's *privacy protection* solutions help to safeguard the personal data collected by government systems. SRA's services include privacy training for government personnel, developing privacy impact assessments, integrating privacy policy across a federal agency or department, and offering strategic consulting on business processes that reinforce privacy. SRA has provided support and advice on privacy and related issues to several federal government agencies. For example, SRA has helped DHHS to determine the appropriate measures for protecting employment information and for complying with federal privacy requirements.[1]

Federal Government Information Security Requirements

Associated with SRA's many services and solutions is the requirement that all federal agencies and their contractors must comply with government security regulations. Since 2002, compliance with the provisions set forth in the Federal Information Security Management Act (FISMA) has been mandatory and is treated as a matter of national security.

Federal Information Security Management Act

FISMA was enacted into law on December 17, 2002, as Title III of the E-Government Act of 2002 (Public Law 107-347). FISMA requires each federal government agency to develop, document, and implement an agency-wide security program to protect the agency's information and information systems, including those provided or managed by another organization (e.g., another federal agency or contractor).[7] Each information security program contains eight requirements.

1. Periodic risk assessments to gauge the risk and magnitude of harm that could result from the unauthorized access, use, disclosure, disruption, modification, or destruction of information or information systems[8];

2. Risk-based policies and procedures that cost-effectively mitigate information security risks and ensure that security is addressed throughout the life cycle of each information system[8];

3. System security plans that provide an overview of the security requirements of the information system, describe the controls in place or planned, and delineate the responsibilities and expected behavior of all users[8];

4. Information security training to inform all users (e.g., federal agency personnel and contractors) of the risks associated with their activities and their responsibilities in complying with the agency's risk-based policies and procedures[8];

5. Periodic testing and evaluation of all security policies, procedures, and practices, which must be done at least once each year[8];

6. Remedial action plans (also referred to as Plans of Action and Milestones) that identify the weaknesses in information security policies and procedures, estimate the resources needed to

resolve these deficiencies, and describe the status of existing corrective actions[8];

7. Security incident procedures to detect, report, and respond to security incidents, to mitigate the risks associated with these incidents before substantial damage is done, and to notify and consult with others (e.g., law enforcement) when necessary[8]; and

8. Continuity of operations plans and procedures that provide specific instructions for restoring critical systems, including the use of alternative processing facilities.[8]

In addition, each federal agency must maintain an inventory of major information systems operated or controlled by the agency, including the identification of all interfaces between each system and all other systems or networks.[8]

FISMA requires each federal agency to submit an annual report to the Office of Management and Budget (OMB). The report must describe the adequacy of the agency's information security program with respect to the eight FISMA requirements identified. OMB, in turn, must annually report to Congress on each federal agency's level of compliance with FISMA.[8] Based on the report submitted to Congress, the Government Reform Committee issues its annual Federal Computer Security Report Card (Table 5-4).

Federal Government Information Security Standards and Controls

To provide guidance for the information security program framework established by FISMA, significant responsibility is assigned to the National Institute of Standards and Technology (NIST). Under FISMA, NIST's statutory requirements include the development of categorization standards and minimum security control requirements for federal information and information systems. To fulfill these specific requirements, NIST published two documents: *Federal Information Processing Standard* (FIPS) *Publication 199* and *NIST Special Publication 800-53.*

TABLE 5-4 2004 Federal Computer Security Report Card
Government-Wide Grade for 2004: D+

FEDERAL GOVERNMENT AGENCY	2004	2003
Agency for International Development	A+	C-
Department of Agriculture	F	F
Department of Commerce	F	C
Department of Defense	D	D
Department of Education	C	C+
Department of Energy	F	F
Department of Health and Human Services	F	F
Department of Homeland Security	F	F
Department of the Interior	C+	F
Department of Justice	B-	F
Department of Labor	B-	B
Department of State	D+	F
Department of Transportation	A-	D+
Department of the Treasury	D+	D
Department of Veterans Affairs	F	C
Environmental Protection Agency	B	C
General Services Administration	C+	D
Housing and Urban Development	F	F
National Aeronautics and Space Administration	D-	D-
National Science Foundation	C+	A-
Nuclear Regulatory Commission	B+	A
Office of Personnel Management	C-	D-
Small Business Administration	D-	C-
Social Security Administration	B	B+

Source: Government Reform Committee, February 16, 2005. Available:
http://reform.house.gov/UploadedFiles/2004%20Computer%20Security%20Report
%20card%202%20years.pdf.

Both documents are critical to federal government agencies as they work to achieve FISMA compliance.

FIPS Publication 199, "Standards for Security Categorization of Federal Information and Information Systems," was published in February 2004. It defines three levels of potential impact on organizations or individuals if an information security breach occurs:

- *Low*—if the loss of confidentiality, integrity, or availability has a limited adverse effect on the organization or individuals (e.g., the organization can perform its primary functions at reduced efficiency, there is minor damage to organizational assets, there is minor financial loss, or there is minor harm to individuals)[9];
- *Moderate*—if the loss of confidentiality, integrity, or availability has a serious adverse effect on the organization or individuals (e.g., the organization can barely perform its primary functions, there is significant damage to organizational assets, there is significant financial loss, or there is significant harm to individuals but there is no loss of life and there are no life-threatening injuries)[9]; and
- *High*—if the loss of confidentiality, integrity, or availability has a severe or catastrophic effect on the organization or individuals (e.g., the organization cannot perform one or more of its primary functions, there is major damage to organizational assets, there is major financial loss, or there is catastrophic harm to individuals that includes loss of life or life-threatening injuries).[9]

Categorizing an agency's information and information systems is a function of the security objective (confidentiality, integrity, or availability) and the potential impact if an information security breach occurs (low, moderate, or high).[10]

NIST Special Publication 800-53, "Recommended Security Controls for Federal Information Systems," was published in February 2005.[11] It provides guidelines for selecting and specifying security controls for information and information systems that have been categorized in accordance with FIPS Publication 199. The security controls are organized into three general classes (management, operational, and technical), which are intended to correspond to the major sections of a security plan. Among the three classes there are a total of seventeen families, which represent the minimum security control requirements for each class. Each family contains a list of specific security controls related to the security function of the family,[12] shown in Table 5-5.

Facilitating Information Security Compliance

Complying with FISMA regulations is a complex task that requires each federal agency to conduct an in-depth security assessment of its information and information systems. To facilitate this process, SRA worked with the Environmental Protection Agency to develop a web-based risk assessment tool called ASSERT (Automated Security Self-Evaluation and Remediation Tracking). ASSERT is an automated self-assessment guide for federal information and information systems. It can be used to monitor the status of information assets and IT systems, generate remediation plans, track risk mitigation activities, monitor progress on the resolution of vulnerabilities, and produce the reports required for OMB.

ASSERT's technology is based on a web-enabled Oracle database that uses Macromedia's ColdFusion for the user interface.[13] ASSERT's capabilities are based on its assessment questions, which incorporate the security categorizations and minimum control requirements described in NIST documents.[14] The software's assessment questions are separated into three classes and seventeen control objectives,[15] as shown in Table 5-6. The assessment questions are used for security program review to determine whether the agency has the necessary security policies and procedures in place, and to determine whether the procedures and security controls have been implemented, tested, and fully integrated into a comprehensive information security program.

TABLE 5-5 Minimum Security Control Requirements

CLASS	FAMILY	SPECIFIC SECURITY CONTROLS
Management	Risk Assessment	1. Risk Assessment Policy and Procedures 2. Security Categorization 3. Risk Assessment 4. Risk Assessment Update 5. Vulnerability Scanning
	Planning	1. Security Planning Policy and Procedures 2. System Security Plan 3. System Security Plan Update 4. Rules of Behavior 5. Privacy Impact Assessment
	System and Services Acquisition	1. System and Services Acquisition Policy and Procedures 2. Allocation of Resources 3. Life Cycle Support 4. Acquisitions 5. Information System Documentation 6. Software Usage Restrictions 7. User Installed Software 8. Security Design Principles 9. Outsourced Information System Services 10. Developer Configuration Management 11. Developer Security Testing
	Certification, Accreditation, and Security Assessments	1. Certification, Accreditation, and Security Assessment Policies and Procedures 2. Security Assessments 3. Information System Connections 4. Security Certification 5. Plan of Action and Milestones 6. Security Accreditation 7. Continuous Monitoring
Operational	Personnel Security	1. Personnel Security Policy and Procedures 2. Position Categorization 3. Personnel Screening

(continues)

TABLE 5-5 Minimum Security Control Requirements *(continued)*

CLASS	FAMILY	SPECIFIC SECURITY CONTROLS
		4. Personnel Termination
		5. Personnel Transfer
		6. Access Agreements
		7. Third-Party Personnel Security
		8. Personnel Sanctions
	Physical and Environmental Protection	1. Physical and Environmental Protection Policy and Procedures
		2. Physical Access Authorizations
		3. Physical Access Control
		4. Access Control for Transmission Medium
		5. Access Control for Display Medium
		6. Monitoring Physical Access
		7. Visitor Control
		8. Access Logs
		9. Power Equipment and Power Cabling
		10. Emergency Shutoff
		11. Emergency Power
		12. Emergency Lighting
		13. Fire Protection
		14. Temperature and Humidity Controls
		15. Water Damage Protection
		16. Delivery and Removal
		17. Alternate Work Site
	Contingency Planning	1. Contingency Planning Policy and Procedures
		2. Contingency Plan
		3. Contingency Training
		4. Contingency Plan Testing
		5. Contingency Plan Update
		6. Alternate Storage Sites
		7. Alternate Processing Sites
		8. Telecommunications Services
		9. Information System Backup
		10. Information System Recovery and Reconstitution

TABLE 5-5 Minimum Security Control Requirements *(continued)*

CLASS	FAMILY	SPECIFIC SECURITY CONTROLS
	Configuration Management	1. Configuration Management Policy and Procedures 2. Baseline Configuration 3. Configuration Change Control 4. Monitoring Configuration Changes 5. Access Restrictions for Change 6. Configuration Settings 7. Least Functionality
	Maintenance	1. System Maintenance Policy and Procedures 2. Periodic Maintenance 3. Maintenance Tools 4. Remote Maintenance 5. Maintenance Personnel 6. Timely Maintenance
	System and Information Integrity	1. System and Information Integrity Policy and Procedures 2. Flaw Remediation 3. Malicious Code Protection 4. Intrusion Detection Tools and Techniques 5. Security Alerts and Advisories 6. Security Functionality Verification 7. Software and Information Integrity 8. Spam and Spyware Protection 9. Information Input Restrictions 10. Information Input Accuracy, Completeness, and Validity 11. Error Handling 12. Information Output Handling and Retention
	Media Protection	1. Media Protection Policy and Procedures 2. Media Access 3. Media Labeling 4. Media Storage 5. Media Transport 6. Media Sanitization 7. Media Destruction and Disposal

(continues)

TABLE 5-5 **Minimum Security Control Requirements** *(continued)*

CLASS	FAMILY	SPECIFIC SECURITY CONTROLS
	Incident Response	1. Incident Response Policy and Procedures 2. Incident Response Training 3. Incident Response Testing 4. Incident Handling 5. Incident Monitoring 6. Incident Reporting 7. Incident Response Assistance
	Awareness and Training	1. Security Awareness and Training Policy and Procedures 2. Security Awareness 3. Security Training 4. Security Training Records
Technical	Identification and Authentication	1. Identification and Authentication Policy and Procedures 2. User Identification and Authentication 3. Device Identification and Authentication 4. Identifier Management 5. Authenticator Management 6. Authenticator Feedback 7. Cryptographic Module Authentication
	Access Control	1. Access Control Policy and Procedures 2. Account Management 3. Access Enforcement 4. Information Flow Enforcement 5. Separation of Duties 6. Least Privilege 7. Unsuccessful Login Attempts 8. System Use Notification 9. Previous Logon Notification 10. Concurrent Session Control 11. Session Lock 12. Session Termination

TABLE 5-5 Minimum Security Control Requirements *(continued)*

CLASS	FAMILY	SPECIFIC SECURITY CONTROLS
		13. Supervision and Review— Access Control
		14. Permitted Actions Without Identification or Authentication
		15. Automated Marking
		16. Automated Labeling
		17. Remote Access
		18. Wireless Access Restrictions
		19. Access Control for Portable and Mobile Systems
		20. Personally Owned Information Systems
	Audit and Accountability	1. Audit and Accountability Policy and Procedures
		2. Auditable Events
		3. Content of Audit Records
		4. Audit Storage Capacity
		5. Audit Processing
		6. Audit Monitoring, Analysis, and Reporting
		7. Audit Reduction and Report Generation
		8. Time Stamps
		9. Protection of Audit Information
		10. Nonrepudiation
		11. Audit Retention
	System and Communications Protection	1. System and Communications Protection Policy and Procedures
		2. Application Partitioning
		3. Security Function Isolation
		4. Information Remnants
		5. Denial of Service Protection
		6. Resource Priority
		7. Boundary Protection
		8. Transmission Integrity
		9. Transmission Confidentiality
		10. Network Disconnect
		11. Trusted Path

(continues)

TABLE 5-5 Minimum Security Control Requirements *(continued)*

CLASS	FAMILY	SPECIFIC SECURITY CONTROLS
		12. Cryptographic Key Establishment and Management
		13. Use of Validated Cryptography
		14. Public Access Protections
		15. Collaborative Computing
		16. Transmission of Security Parameters
		17. Public Key Infrastructure Certificates
		18. Mobile Code
		19. Voice Over Internet Protocol

Source: U.S. Department of Commerce, National Institute of Standards and Technology, Special Publication 800-53, "Recommended Security Controls for Federal Information Systems," February 2005. Available: http://csrc.nist.gov/publications/nistpubs/800-53/SP800-53.pdf.

TABLE 5-6 Assessment Questions

MANAGEMENT CONTROLS

1. Risk Management

  1.1. Is risk periodically assessed?

    1.1.1 Is the current system configuration documented, including links to other systems?

    1.1.2 Are risk assessments performed and documented on a regular basis or whenever the system, facilities, or other conditions change?

    1.1.3 Has data sensitivity and integrity of the data been considered?

    1.1.4 Have threat sources, both natural and manmade, been identified?

    1.1.5 Has a list of known system vulnerabilities, system flaws, or weaknesses that could be exploited by the threat sources been developed and maintained current?

TABLE 5-6 Assessment Questions *(continued)*

 1.1.6 Has an analysis been conducted that determines whether the security requirements in place adequately mitigate vulnerabilities?

 1.2. Do program officials understand the risk to systems under their control and determine the acceptable level of risk?

 1.2.1 Are final risk determinations and related management approvals documented and maintained on file?

 1.2.2 Has a mission/business impact analysis been conducted?

 1.2.3 Have additional controls been identified to sufficiently mitigate identified risks?

2. Review of Security Controls

 2.1. Have the security controls of the system and interconnected systems been reviewed?

 2.1.1 Has the system and all network boundaries been subjected to periodic reviews?

 2.1.2 Has an independent review been performed when a significant change occurred?

 2.1.3 Are routine self-assessments conducted?

 2.1.4 Are tests and examinations of key controls routinely made (i.e., network scans, analyses of router and switch settings, penetration testing)?

 2.1.5 Are security alerts and security incidents analyzed and remedial actions taken?

 2.2. Does management ensure that corrective actions are effectively implemented?

 2.2.1 Is there an effective and timely process for reporting significant weakness and ensuring effective remedial action?

3. Life Cycle

 3.1. Has a system development life cycle methodology been developed?

 3.1.1 Is the sensitivity of the system determined?

 3.1.2 Does the business case document the resources required for adequately securing the system?

 3.1.3 Does the Investment Review Board ensure any investment request includes the security resources needed?

(continues)

TABLE 5-6 Assessment Questions *(continued)*

3.1.4 Are authorizations for software modifications documented and maintained?

3.1.5 Does the budget request include the security resources required for the system?

3.1.6 During system design, are security requirements identified?

3.1.7 Was an initial risk assessment performed to determine security requirements?

3.1.8 Is there a written agreement with program officials on the security controls employed and residual risk?

3.1.9 Are security controls consistent with and an integral part of the IT architecture of the agency?

3.1.10 Are the appropriate security controls with associated evaluation and test procedures developed before the procurement action?

3.1.11 Do the solicitation documents (e.g., Request for Proposals) include security requirements and evaluation/test procedures?

3.1.12 Do the requirements in the solicitation documents permit updating security controls as new threats/vulnerabilities are identified and as new technologies are implemented?

3.2. Are changes controlled as programs progress through testing to final approval?

3.2.1 Are design reviews and system tests run prior to placing the system in production?

3.2.2 Are the test results documented?

3.2.3 Is certification testing of security controls conducted and documented?

3.2.4 If security controls were added since development, has the system documentation been modified to include them?

3.2.5 If security controls were added since development, have the security controls been tested and the system recertified?

TABLE 5-6 Assessment Questions *(continued)*

3.2.6 Has the application undergone a technical evaluation to ensure that it meets applicable federal laws, regulations, policies, guidelines, and standards?

3.2.7 Does the system have written authorization to operate either on an interim basis with planned corrective action or full authorization?

3.2.8 Has a system security plan been developed and approved?

3.2.9 If the system connects to other systems, have controls been established and disseminated to the owners of the interconnected systems?

3.2.10 Is the system security plan kept current?

3.2.11 Are official electronic records properly disposed/archived?

3.2.12 Is information or media purged, overwritten, degaussed, or destroyed when disposed or used elsewhere?

3.2.13 Is a record kept of who implemented the disposal actions and verified that the information or media was sanitized?

4. Authorize Processing (Certification and Accreditation)

4.1. Has the system been certified/recertified and authorized to process (accredited)?

4.1.1 Has a technical and/or security evaluation been completed or conducted when a significant change occurred?

4.1.2 Has a risk assessment been conducted when a significant change occurred?

4.1.3 Have Rules of Behavior been established and signed by users?

4.1.4 Has a contingency plan been developed and tested?

4.1.5 Has a system security plan been developed, updated, and reviewed?

4.1.6 Are in-place controls operating as intended?

4.1.7 Are the planned and in-place controls consistent with the identified risks and the system and data sensitivity?

(continues)

TABLE 5-6 Assessment Questions *(continued)*

      4.1.8   Has management authorized interconnections to all systems (including systems owned and operated by another program, agency, organization, or contractor)?

    4.2. Is the system operating on an interim authority to process in accordance with specified agency procedures?

      4.2.1   Has management initiated prompt action to correct deficiencies?

5. System Security Plan

    5.1. Is a system security plan documented for the system and all interconnected systems if the boundary controls are ineffective?

      5.1.1   Is the system security plan approved by key affected parties and management?

      5.1.2   Does the plan contain the topics prescribed in NIST Special Publication 800-18?

      5.1.3   Is a summary of the plan incorporated into the strategic IRM plan?

    5.2. Is the plan kept current?

      5.2.1   Is the plan reviewed periodically and adjusted to reflect current conditions and risks?

OPERATIONAL CONTROLS

6. Personnel Security

    6.1. Are duties separated to ensure least privilege and individual accountability?

      6.1.1   Are all positions reviewed for sensitivity level?

      6.1.2   Are there documented job descriptions that accurately reflect assigned duties and responsibilities and that segregate duties?

      6.1.3   Are sensitive functions divided among different individuals?

      6.1.4   Are distinct systems support functions performed by different individuals?

      6.1.5   Are mechanisms in place for holding users responsible for their actions?

TABLE 5-6 Assessment Questions *(continued)*

6.1.6 Are regularly scheduled vacations and periodic job/shift rotations required?

6.1.7 Are hiring, transfer, and termination procedures established?

6.1.8 Is there a process for requesting, establishing, issuing, and closing user accounts?

6.2. Is appropriate background screening for assigned positions completed prior to granting access?

6.2.1 Are individuals who are authorized to bypass significant technical and operational controls screened prior to access and periodically thereafter?

6.2.2 Are confidentiality or security agreements required for employees assigned to work with sensitive information?

6.2.3 When controls cannot adequately protect the information, are individuals screened prior to access?

6.2.4 Are there conditions for allowing system access prior to completion of screening?

7. Physical and Environmental Protection

7.1. Have adequate physical security controls been implemented that are commensurate with the risks of physical damage or access?

7.1.1 Is access to facilities controlled through the use of guards, identification badges, or entry devices such as key cards or biometrics?

7.1.2 Does management regularly review the list of persons with physical access to sensitive facilities?

7.1.3 Are deposits and withdrawals of tapes and other storage media from the library authorized and logged?

7.1.4 Are keys or other access devices needed to enter the computer room and tape/media library?

7.1.5 Are unused keys or other entry devices secured?

7.1.6 Do emergency exit and re-entry procedures ensure that only authorized personnel are allowed to re-enter after fire drills, etc.?

(continues)

TABLE 5-6 Assessment Questions *(continued)*

7.1.7 Are visitors to sensitive areas signed in and escorted?

7.1.8 Are entry codes changed periodically?

7.1.9 Are physical accesses monitored through audit trails and apparent security violations investigated and remedial action taken?

7.1.10 Is suspicious access activity investigated and appropriate action taken?

7.1.11 Are visitors, contractors, and maintenance personnel authenticated through the use of preplanned appointments and identification checks?

7.1.12 Are appropriate fire suppression and prevention devices installed and working?

7.1.13 Are fire ignition sources, such as failures of electronic devices or wiring, improper storage materials, and the possibility of arson, reviewed periodically?

7.1.14 Are heating and air-conditioning systems regularly maintained?

7.1.15 Is there a redundant air-cooling system?

7.1.16 Are electric power distribution, heating plants, water, sewage, and other utilities periodically reviewed for risk of failure?

7.1.17 Are building plumbing lines known and do not endanger system?

7.1.18 Has an uninterruptible power supply or backup generator been provided?

7.1.19 Have controls been implemented to mitigate other disasters, such as floods, earthquakes, etc.?

7.2. Is data protected from interception?

7.2.1 Are computer monitors located to eliminate viewing by unauthorized persons?

7.2.2 Is physical access to data transmission lines controlled?

7.3. Are mobile and portable systems protected?

7.3.1 Are sensitive data files encrypted on all portable systems?

7.3.2 Are portable systems stored securely?

TABLE 5-6 Assessment Questions *(continued)*

8. Production, Input/Output Controls
   8.1. Is there user support?
      8.1.1 Is there a help desk or group that offers advice?
   8.2. Are there media controls?
      8.2.1 Are there processes to ensure that unauthorized individuals cannot read, copy, alter, or steal printed or electronic information?
      8.2.2 Are there processes for ensuring that only authorized users pick up, receive, or deliver input and output information and media?
      8.2.3 Are audit trails used for receipt of sensitive inputs/outputs?
      8.2.4 Are controls in place for transporting or mailing media or printed output?
      8.2.5 Is there internal/external labeling for sensitivity?
      8.2.6 Is there external labeling with special handling instructions?
      8.2.7 Are audit trails kept for inventory management?
      8.2.8 Is media sanitized for reuse?
      8.2.9 Is damaged media stored and/or destroyed?
      8.2.10 Is hardcopy media shredded or destroyed when no longer needed?
9. Contingency Planning
   9.1. Have the most critical and sensitive operations and their supporting computer resources been identified?
      9.1.1 Are critical data files and operations identified and the frequency of file backup documented?
      9.1.2 Are resources supporting critical operations identified?
      9.1.3 Have processing priorities been established and approved by management?
   9.2. Has a comprehensive contingency plan been developed and documented?
      9.2.1 Is the plan approved by key affected parties?
      9.2.2 Are responsibilities for recovery assigned?
      9.2.3 Are there detailed instructions for restoring operations?

(continues)

TABLE 5-6 Assessment Questions *(continued)*

9.2.4 Is there an alternate processing site; if so, is there a contract or interagency agreement in place?

9.2.5 Is the location of stored backups identified?

9.2.6 Are backup files created on a prescribed basis and rotated off site often enough to avoid disruption if current files are damaged?

9.2.7 Is system and application documentation maintained at the off-site location?

9.2.8 Are all system defaults reset after being restored from a backup?

9.2.9 Are the backup storage site and alternate site geographically removed from the primary site and physically protected?

9.2.10 Has the contingency plan been distributed to all appropriate personnel?

9.3. Are tested contingency/disaster recovery plans in place?

9.3.1 Is an up-to-date copy of the plan stored securely off site?

9.3.2 Are employees trained in their roles and responsibilities?

9.3.3 Is the plan periodically tested and readjusted as appropriate?

10. Hardware and System Software Maintenance

10.1. Is access limited to system software and hardware?

10.1.1 Are restrictions in place on who performs maintenance and repair activities?

10.1.2 Is access to all program libraries restricted and controlled?

10.1.3 Are there on-site and off-site maintenance procedures (e.g., escort of maintenance personnel, sanitization of devices removed from the site)?

10.1.4 Is the operating system configured to prevent circumvention of the security software and application controls?

10.1.5 Are up-to-date procedures in place for using and monitoring use of system utilities?

10.2. Are all new and revised hardware and software authorized, tested, and approved before implementation?

TABLE 5-6 Assessment Questions *(continued)*

10.2.1 Is an impact analysis conducted to determine the effect of proposed changes on existing security controls, including the required training needed to implement the control?

10.2.2 Are system components tested, documented, and approved (operating system, utility, applications) prior to promotion to production?

10.2.3 Are software change request forms used to document requests and related approvals?

10.2.4 Are there detailed system specifications prepared and reviewed by management?

10.2.5 Is the type of test data to be used specified—live or made up?

10.2.6 Are default settings of security features set to the most restrictive mode?

10.2.7 Are there software distribution implementation orders including effective date provided to all locations?

10.2.8 Is there version control?

10.2.9 Are programs labeled and inventoried?

10.2.10 Are the distribution and implementation of new or revised software documented and reviewed?

10.2.11 Are emergency change procedures documented and approved by management, either prior to the change or after the fact?

10.2.12 Are contingency plans and other associated documentation updated to reflect system changes?

10.2.13 Is the use of copyrighted software or shareware and personally owned software/equipment documented?

10.3. Are systems managed to reduce vulnerabilities?

10.3.1 Are systems periodically reviewed to identify and, when possible, eliminate unnecessary services (e.g., FTP, HTTP, mainframe supervisor calls)?

10.3.2 Are systems periodically reviewed for known vulnerabilities and software patches promptly installed?

(continues)

TABLE 5-6 Assessment Questions *(continued)*

11. Data Integrity

    11.1. Is virus detection and elimination software installed and activated?

        11.1.1 Are virus signature files routinely updated?

        11.1.2 Are virus scans automatic?

    11.2. Are data integrity and validation controls used to provide assurance that the information has not been altered and the system functions as intended?

        11.2.1 Are reconciliation routines used by applications— checksums, hash totals, record counts?

        11.2.2 Is inappropriate or unusual activity reported, investigated, and appropriate actions taken?

        11.2.3 Are procedures in place to determine compliance with password policies?

        11.2.4 Are integrity verification programs used by applications to look for evidence of data tampering, errors, and omissions?

        11.2.5 Are intrusion detection tools installed on the system?

        11.2.6 Are the intrusion detection reports routinely reviewed and suspected incidents handled accordingly?

        11.2.7 Is system performance monitoring used to analyze system performance logs in real time to look for availability problems, including active attacks?

        11.2.8 Is penetration testing performed on the system?

        11.2.9 Is message authentication used?

12. Documentation

    12.1. Is there sufficient documentation that explains how software/hardware is to be used?

        12.1.1 Is there vendor-supplied documentation of purchased software?

        12.1.2 Is there vendor-supplied documentation of purchased hardware?

        12.1.3 Is there application documentation for in-house applications?

TABLE 5-6 Assessment Questions *(continued)*

12.1.4   Are there network diagrams and documentation on setups of routers and switches?

12.1.5   Are there software and hardware testing procedures and results?

12.1.6   Are there standard operating procedures for all the topic areas covered in this document?

12.1.7   Are there user manuals?

12.1.8   Are there emergency procedures?

12.1.9   Are there backup procedures?

12.2.   Are there formal security and operational procedures documented?

12.2.1   Is there a system security plan?

12.2.2   Is there a contingency plan?

12.2.3   Are there written agreements regarding how data is shared between interconnected systems?

12.2.4   Are there risk assessment reports?

12.2.5   Are there certification and accreditation documents and a statement authorizing the system to process?

13. Security Awareness, Training, and Education

13.1.   Have employees received adequate training to fulfill their security responsibilities?

13.1.1   Have employees received a copy of the Rules of Behavior?

13.1.2   Are employee training and professional development documented and monitored?

13.1.3   Is there mandatory annual refresher training?

13.1.4   Are methods employed to make employees aware of security (i.e., posters, booklets)?

13.1.5   Have employees received a copy of or have easy access to agency security procedures and policies?

14. Incident Response Capability

14.1.   Is there a capability to provide help to users when a security incident occurs in the system?

14.1.1   Is a formal incident response capability available?

(continues)

TABLE 5-6 Assessment Questions *(continued)*

14.1.2 Is there a process for reporting incidents?

14.1.3 Are incidents monitored and tracked until resolved?

14.1.4 Are personnel trained to recognize and handle incidents?

14.1.5 Are alerts/advisories received and responded to?

14.1.6 Is there a process to modify incident handling procedures and control techniques after an incident occurs?

14.2. Is incident-related information shared with appropriate organizations?

14.2.1 Is incident information and common vulnerabilities or threats shared with owners of interconnected systems?

14.2.2 Is incident information shared with FedCIRC concerning incidents and common vulnerabilities and threats?

14.2.3 Is incident information reported to FedCIRC, NIPC, and local law enforcement when necessary?

TECHNICAL CONTROLS

15. Identification and Authentication

15.1. Are users individually authenticated via passwords, tokens, or other devices?

15.1.1 Is a current list maintained and approved of authorized users and their access?

15.1.2 Are digital signatures used and conform to FIPS 186-2?

15.1.3 Are access scripts with embedded passwords prohibited?

15.1.4 Is emergency and temporary access authorized?

15.1.5 Are personnel files matched with user accounts to ensure that terminated or transferred individuals do not retain system access?

15.1.6 Are passwords changed at least every ninety days or earlier if needed?

15.1.7 Are passwords unique and difficult to guess (e.g., do passwords require alphanumeric, upper/lower case, and special characters)?

TABLE 5-6 Assessment Questions *(continued)*

15.1.8 Are inactive user identifications disabled after a specified period of time?

15.1.9 Are passwords not displayed when entered?

15.1.10 Are there procedures in place for handling lost and compromised passwords?

15.1.11 Are passwords distributed securely and users informed not to reveal their passwords to anyone (social engineering)?

15.1.12 Are passwords transmitted and stored using secure protocols/algorithms?

15.1.13 Are vendor-supplied passwords replaced immediately?

15.1.14 Is there a limit to the number of invalid access attempts that may occur for a given user?

15.2. Are access controls enforcing segregation of duties?

15.2.1 Does the system correlate actions to users?

15.2.2 Do data owners periodically review access authorizations to determine whether they remain appropriate?

16. Logical Access Controls

16.1. Do the logical access controls restrict users to authorized transactions and functions?

16.1.1 Can the security controls detect unauthorized access attempts?

16.1.2 Is there access control software that prevents an individual from having all necessary authority or information access to allow fraudulent activity without collusion?

16.1.3 Is access to security software restricted to security administrators?

16.1.4 Do workstations disconnect or screen savers lock system after a specific period of inactivity?

16.1.5 Are inactive users' accounts monitored and removed when not needed?

16.1.6 Are internal security labels (naming conventions) used to control access to specific information types or files?

16.1.7 If encryption is used, does it meet federal standards?

(continues)

TABLE 5-6 Assessment Questions *(continued)*

16.1.8 If encryption is used, are there procedures for key generation, distribution, storage, use, destruction, and archiving?

16.1.9 Is access restricted to files at the logical view or field?

16.1.10 Is access monitored to identify apparent security violations and are such events investigated?

16.2. Are there logical controls over network access?

16.2.1 Has communication software been implemented to restrict access through specific terminals?

16.2.2 Are insecure protocols (e.g., UDP, ftp) disabled?

16.2.3 Have all vendor-supplied default security parameters been reinitialized to more secure settings?

16.2.4 Are there controls that restrict remote access to the system?

16.2.5 Are network activity logs maintained and reviewed?

16.2.6 Does the network connection automatically disconnect at the end of a session?

16.2.7 Are trust relationships among hosts and external entities appropriately restricted?

16.2.8 Is dial-in access monitored?

16.2.9 Is access to telecommunications hardware or facilities restricted and monitored?

16.2.10 Are firewalls or secure gateways installed?

16.2.11 If firewalls are installed, do they comply with firewall policy and rules?

16.2.12 Are guest and anonymous accounts authorized and monitored?

16.2.13 Is an approved standardized log-on banner displayed on the system warning unauthorized users that they have accessed a U.S. government system and can be punished?

16.2.14 Are sensitive data transmissions encrypted?

16.2.15 Is access to tables defining network options, resources, and operator profiles restricted?

TABLE 5-6 Assessment Questions *(continued)*

    16.3. If the public accesses the system, are there controls implemented to protect the integrity of the application and the confidence of the public?

        16.3.1 Is a privacy policy posted on the Web site?

17. Audit Trails

    17.1. Is activity involving access to and modification of sensitive or critical files logged, monitored, and possible security violations investigated?

        17.1.1 Does the audit trail provide a trace of user actions?

        17.1.2 Can the audit trail support after-the-fact investigations of how, when, and why normal operations ceased?

        17.1.3 Is access to on-line audit logs strictly controlled?

        17.1.4 Are off-line storage of audit logs retained for a period of time, and if so, is access to audit logs strictly controlled?

        17.1.5 Is there separation of duties between security personnel who administer the access control function and those who administer the audit trail?

        17.1.6 Are audit trails reviewed frequently?

        17.1.7 Are automated tools used to review audit records in real time or near real time?

        17.1.8 Is suspicious activity investigated and appropriate action taken?

        17.1.9 Is keystroke monitoring used? If so, are users notified?

Source: U.S. Department of Commerce, National Institute of Standards and Technology Special Publication 800-26, "Security Self-Assessment Guide for Information Technology Systems," November 2001. Available: http://csrc.nist.gov/publications/nistpubs/800-26/sp800-26.pdf.

ASSERT displays each assessment question in context and allows system owners to easily navigate between questions. Once the questions have been answered for the first time, future evaluations require considerably less effort. ASSERT uses the prior year's responses as a baseline to prefill and inherit answers wherever possible, reducing the time required to complete the assessment process to approximately two hours a year.[13]

ASSERT automatically generates remedial action plans based on the assessment answers. It links each remedial action plan to the information asset and to the business unit that owns it, and it identifies the assessment questions that generated each remedial action plan. It also provides the basic steps needed to remediate each identified vulnerability, along with the name of the individual responsible for each step. This makes it easier for managers at each agency to track the progress of their corrective actions.[16]

From the assessment responses, ASSERT creates a centralized database of security data associated with an agency's information systems (e.g., points of contact, date of latest approved security plan, information sensitivity classifications, resource needs). It also identifies risks to those systems, and provides current information on the status of the agency's security controls and remedial action plan initiatives. This information allows responsible managers to know the status of their systems at any point in time, enabling them to quickly institute necessary security improvements.[16]

To simplify the reporting process, ASSERT incorporates the eight information security program requirements mandated by FISMA (periodic risk assessments, risk-based policies and procedures, system security plans, information security training, periodic testing and evaluation of security policies, remedial action plans, security incident procedures, and continuity of operations plans). For each agency system, ASSERT automatically summarizes the data needed to submit OMB reports.[17]

Final Comments

SRA developed ASSERT in 2003 to automate the annual FISMA assessment process for the EPA's Office of Environmental Information. Since that time, SRA has helped the EPA to develop a consortium through which federal agencies could work together on software development. This collaborative approach allows software to be developed and shared among federal agencies in a more efficient and cost-effective manner. The establishment of the consortium allowed ASSERT to become used by other federal agencies, including the Social Security Administration and the General Services Administration.[13] As of September 2005, ASSERT was in the process of being implemented at the Federal Aviation Administration (an agency of the U.S. Department of Transportation). In addition, NIST is in the process of developing an XML schema for NIST FISMA compliance that will facilitate the collaborative, information sharing model pioneered by SRA.[17]

Driven by the demands of FISMA, information security within the federal government is a demanding endeavor requiring teamwork, the sharing of ideas, the application of strong security solutions, and the evolution of standardized practices, all of which must be cost effective.[17] By automating the FISMA compliance process, ASSERT has provided an efficient means for federal agencies to verify their compliance with government information security regulations.

Acknowledgments

SRA, SRA International, Inc., NetOwl, and ORIONMagic are registered trademarks of SRA International, Inc. Blackberry is a registered trademark of Research In Motion. ENERGY STAR is a registered trademark of the Environmental Protection Agency. All rights reserved.

Endnotes

1. U.S. Securities and Exchange Commission, Form 10-K, "Annual Report for the Year Ended June 30, 2005, SRA International, Inc." Available: http://ir.sra.com/phoenix.zhtml?c=131092&p=irol-SEC.
2. Distributive Training Technology Project. Available: http://www.dttp. ngb.army.mil/default.asp.

3. SRA International, Inc., "2004 Annual Report." Available: http://media.corporate-ir.net/media_files/irol/13/131092/reports/SRA2004AR.pdf.

4. A *brownfield* is a property whose expansion, redevelopment, or reuse may be complicated by the presence of a hazardous substance or contaminant. The EPA established the Brownfields Program in 1995 to prevent, assess, clean up, and reuse brownfields. There is considerable information about the EPA's Brownfields Program available at http://www.epa.gov/brownfields/index.html.

5. *Superfund* is the federal government's program to clean up the nation's uncontrolled or abandoned hazardous waste sites. It was established in 1980 with the passage of The Comprehensive Environmental Response, Compensation, and Liability Act (CERCLA). For more information about Superfund and CERCLA, see http://www.epa.gov/superfund/index.htm.

6. The *ENERGY STAR program* is a public/private partnership program between the federal government and industry. The program is designed to help businesses and individuals protect the environment through superior energy efficiency. For more information, see http://www.energystar.gov/index.cfm?c=about.ab_index.

7. E-Government Act of 2002 (H.R. 2458/S. 803; Public Law 107-347). Available: http://thomas.loc.gov/cgi-bin/query/z?c107:H.R.2458.enr.

8. Government Accountability Office, GAO-05-552, "Information Security: Weaknesses Persist at Federal Agencies Despite Progress Made in Implementing Related Statutory Requirements," July 2005. Available: http://www.gao.gov/new.items/d05552.pdf.

9. U.S. Department of Commerce, National Institute of Standards and Technology, Computer Security Division, FIPS PUB 199, "Standards for Security Categorization of Federal Information and Information Systems," February 2004. Available: http://csrc.nist.gov/publications/fips/fips199/FIPS-PUB-199-final.pdf.

10. In June 2004, NIST issued Special Publication 800-60, "Guide for Mapping Types of Information and Information Systems to Security Categories." Available: http://csrc.nist.gov/publications/nistpubs/800-60/SP800-60V1-final.pdf. NIST Special Publication 800-60 provides the criteria used to map information and information systems to the impact levels established in FIPS Publication 199.

11. NIST Special Publication 800-53 is intended to provide interim guidance to federal agencies until FIPS Publication 200, "Minimum Security Requirements for Federal Information and Information Systems," is published in 2006.

12. U.S. Department of Commerce, National Institute of Standards and Technology, Special Publication 800-53, "Recommended Security Controls for Federal Information Systems", February 2005. Available: http://csrc.nist.gov/publications/nistpubs/800-53/SP800-53.pdf.

13. Personal communication with Steve Newburg-Rinn, Director, Civil Government Information Assurance Solutions, SRA International, Inc., July 21, 2005.

14. ASSERT is an automated version of NIST Special Publication 800-26, "Security Self-Assessment Guide for Information Technology Systems." ASSERT incorporates the security categorizations and minimum control requirements described in FIPS Publication 199 and NIST Special Publication 800-53, as set forth in NIST Special Publication 800-26. See also endnote 15.

15. U.S. Department of Commerce, National Institute of Standards and Technology Special Publication 800-26, "Security Self-Assessment Guide for Information Technology Systems," November 2001. Available: http://csrc.nist.gov/publications/nistpubs/800-26/sp800-26.pdf.

16. Steve Newburg-Rinn, "Promoting & Facilitating IT Security Compliance," January 8, 2005. Presentation received from Steve Newburg-Rinn, Director, Civil Government Information Assurance Solutions, SRA International, Inc., July 21, 2005.

17. Personal communication with Mr. Michael Jacobs, Vice President and Director, Cyber and National Security Program, SRA International, Inc., August 31, 2005.

CASE STUDY QUESTIONS

1. Why do you think SRA has chosen to focus its efforts on federal government departments and agencies within the national security market? Explain why this has been a good strategy for SRA.

2. What is open source intelligence? What is the relationship between open source intelligence, national security, and text and data mining software? Why should businesses be concerned about open source intelligence?

3. What are critical infrastructures? List the U.S. critical infrastructure sectors and provide examples of each.

4. Why is improved interoperability between federal agency systems necessary for national security purposes?

5. FISMA replaced the Government Information Security Reform Act (GISRA). Provide an overview of GISRA. Do you think that there are significant differences between FISMA and GISRA?

6. Are the eight FISMA requirements a good model for business information security programs? Explain your answer.

7. In spite of FISMA's mandate to strengthen information security within the federal government, many federal agencies receive low grades on the Federal Computer Security Report Card because of the weaknesses in their information systems and information security programs. Explain why this has happened.

8. What are the differences, in terms of legal regulations and guidance for compliance, between the federal government and industry in managing the security of information and information systems?

9. Compare the classes and families of the minimum security control requirements, shown in Table 5-5, to the classes and control objectives of ASSERT's assessment questions, shown in Table 5-6. How do you explain the discrepancies?

10. Explain how ASSERT's questions could be used by a business to better control its IT systems and to mitigate its security risks.

KEY TERMS

Asynchronous Transfer Mode (ATM): High-speed switching technology capable of transmitting data, video, and voice over the same network.

Availability: Ensuring that information is accessible to authorized parties.

Confidentiality: Preventing the unauthorized disclosure of information.

Configuration Management: Ensuring that only authorized changes are made to the hardware, software, firmware, and documentation of a system throughout the system's life cycle.

Defense Advanced Research Projects Agency (DARPA): Central research and development organization for the U.S. Department of Defense. See http://www.darpa.mil/.

Department of Defense (DoD): Federal department responsible for ensuring national security, created in 1949. It encompasses all military branches (Army, Navy, Marine Corps, Coast Guard, Air Force, National Guard, and Reserves). See http://www.defenselink.mil/home/aboutdod.html.

Department of Health and Human Services (DHHS): Federal department responsible for protecting the health of U.S. citizens and providing essential human services. See http://www.hhs.gov/.

Department of Homeland Security (DHS): Federal department created by the Homeland Security Act of 2002 to prevent terrorist attacks within the United States, to reduce the vulnerability of the United States to terrorism, and to minimize the damage and assist in the recovery from terrorist attacks that occur within the United States. See http://www.dhs.gov/.

Environmental Protection Agency (EPA): Federal department responsible for protecting and improving the natural environment, established in 1970. See http://www.epa.gov/.

Federal Computer Incident Response Capability (FedCIRC): Initiative undertaken by the National Institute of Standards and Technology, the Department of Energy's Computer Incident Advisory Capability, and the Carnegie Mellon Software Engineering Institute's Computer Emergency Response Team Coordination Center, to offer the federal civilian community assistance and guidance in handling computer security-related incidents.

Federal Information Security Management Act (FISMA): Law that requires each federal agency to develop, document, and implement an agency-wide information security program to protect the agency's information and information systems, including those provided or managed by another organization.

Government Accountability Office (GAO): Investigative arm of Congress. Federal agency that studies the federal government's programs and expenditures, evaluates federal programs, audits federal expenditures, issues legal opinions, and recommends actions. Formerly known as the General Accounting Office. See http://www.gao.gov/.

Integrity: Preventing the unauthorized modification or destruction of information.

Internal Revenue Service (IRS): The nation's tax collection agency. The bureau of the Department of the Treasury responsible for administering the Internal Revenue Code enacted by Congress. See http://www.irs.gov/.

National Infrastructure Protection Center (NIPC): Created in 1998 to provide timely warnings of intentional threats to the nation's critical infrastructures, provide comprehensive analyses of these threats, and support law enforcement investigation and response activities. Originally an interagency center within the Federal Bureau of Investigation, it is now part of the Department of Homeland Security Information Analysis and Infrastructure Protection directorate.

National Institute of Standards and Technology (NIST): Federal agency within the U.S. Department of Commerce's Technology Administration. Founded in 1901 as the nation's first federal physical science research laboratory. Responsible for developing and applying measurements, standards and technology to enhance productivity and facilitate trade. See http://www.nist.gov/.

National Institutes of Health (NIH): Responsible for conducting and supporting medical research. An agency of the U.S. Department of Health and Human Services. See http://www.nih.gov/.

Office of Management and Budget (OMB): Responsible for assisting the President in developing and implementing budget, program, management, and regulatory policies. See http://www.whitehouse.gov/omb/.

Penetration Testing: Method of evaluating the security of a system by attempting to circumvent the security features of the system. Testing is carried out from the position of a potential attacker.

Public Key Infrastructure (PKI): Integrated set of services and tools for creating, using, and managing public key-based applications, including the use of asymmetric (public key) cryptography, digital certificates, and certification authorities.

Radio Frequency Identification (RFID): Wireless technology that allows an object to be identified at a distance. A tag is used to store data that can be used to identify the object. The tag is affixed to the object, and it transmits the stored data upon receipt of the radio signal from a reading device.

Risk Assessment: Process of analyzing the threats to, and vulnerabilities of, a system, and evaluating the possible impact and probability of occurrence associated with each potential loss event.

Trusted Path: Mechanism by which the user is assured that she or he is directly communicating with the intended system.

U.S. Agency for International Development (USAID): Independent federal government agency that provides economic, development, and humanitarian assistance around the world in support of U.S. foreign policy goals. See http://www.usaid.gov/.

U.S. Department of Agriculture (USDA): Federal department responsible for the safety of meat, poultry, and egg products, founded in 1862. See http://www.usda.gov/.

U.S. Department of Agriculture (USDA) Forest Service: Responsible for managing public lands in national forests and grasslands, established in 1905. The Forest Service is an agency of the U.S. Department of Agriculture. See http://www.fs.fed.us/.

Vulnerability Analysis: Systematic examination to identify exploitable weaknesses in a system, in the use of the system, its procedures, and its internal controls.

FBI NEW HAVEN FIELD OFFICE—COMPUTER ANALYSIS AND RESPONSE TEAM:

TRACKING A COMPUTER INTRUDER

A company can be a victim of a computer intrusion without its knowledge. This happened to a Connecticut e-commerce company, whose customers received e-mail requests for additional financial information shortly after they had ordered products through the company's Web site. Although the e-mails appeared to be legitimate, they had not been sent from the company. Fearing criminal activity, the company responded by contacting the Federal Bureau of Investigation (FBI) New Haven field office.

This case study describes the methods and processes used by the FBI New Haven field office to locate an intruder who hacked into the company's daily order file and stole customer order information, including credit card numbers. To provide necessary background information, the case study begins with an overview of the FBI, the FBI Laboratory, the Computer Analysis and Response Team, and the FBI New Haven field office.

Federal Bureau of Investigation—Overview

The FBI is the investigative arm of the Department of Justice and the United States' top law enforcement agency. Established in 1908, the Bureau of Investigation had thirty-four agents who were responsible for investigating violations of national laws in banking, naturalization, bankruptcy, antitrust, and land fraud. Over the years, the agency grew in size and magnitude, and its mission and strategic priorities changed in response to the actions and events of the times. Today, the FBI has more than 28,000 employees, and its top three priorities are to protect the United States from terrorist attacks, to counter foreign intelligence operations against the United States, and to protect the United States against cyber-based attacks and high-technology crimes. Table 6-1 summarizes the FBI's growth and change of mandate from its establishment to present day.

FBI headquarters in Washington, D.C., provides administrative support and direction for all FBI operations and investigations. Its four operational divisions (Counterterrorism Division, Counterintelligence Division, Cyber Division, and Criminal Investigative Division) offer support services to the FBI's field offices, satellite offices (referred to as *resident agencies*), and foreign liaison offices (referred to as *Legal Attaché offices* or *Legats*).

The intelligence and investigative work of the FBI is conducted out of its fifty-six field offices and the 400 resident agencies that report to the field offices. Each field office operates with a significant amount of autonomy from FBI headquarters, establishing its own priorities based on what it believes to be the most significant threats to its particular territory. The FBI's forty-five Legats support investigations and operations around the world.[1]

FBI Laboratory and CART

The FBI Laboratory is one of the largest and most comprehensive forensic laboratories in the world. Established in 1932 to provide forensic expertise to law enforcement agencies, the laboratory was established as

TABLE 6-1 Summary of Growth and Change of Mandate

Years	Name	Employees (*n*)	Key Mandates
1908–1910	Bureau of Investigation	34 (9 detectives, 13 civil rights investigators, 12 accountants)	Investigate violations of laws involving national banking, bankruptcy, naturalization, antitrust, and land fraud
1910–1921	Bureau of Investigation	> 600 (including approximately 300 special agents)	Investigate violations of the Mann Act, Espionage Act, Selective Service Act, and Sabotage Act Investigate enemy aliens and criminals who evaded the law by crossing state lines
1921–1932	Bureau of Investigation; renamed United States Bureau of Investigation in 1932	> 1,500 (including > 450 special agents)	Investigate gangsters Track criminals by means of identification records (e.g., fingerprint matching) Compile uniform crime statistics for the United States
1932–1939	United States Bureau of Investigation; renamed Division of Investigation in 1933; renamed Federal Bureau of Investigation in 1935	> 7,000 (including approximately 1,000 special agents)	Lead the national campaign against rampant crime Investigate kidnappings Arrest gangsters and criminals who crossed state lines
1939–1945	Federal Bureau of Investigation	> 13,000 (including approximately 4,000 special agents)	Lead war-related investigations (e.g., investigate fascist and communist groups in the United States; investigate acts of subversion, sabotage, and espionage; investigate potential threats to national security; locate draft evaders and deserters)

(continues)

TABLE 6-1 Summary of Growth and Change of Mandate *(continued)*

YEARS	NAME	EMPLOYEES (*n*)	KEY MANDATES
			Participate in intelligence collection using the Bureau's Laboratory
			Carry out civil rights and traditional criminal investigations
1945–1973	Federal Bureau of Investigation	> 16,000 (including approximately 6,700 special agents)	Investigate acts of subversion, sabotage, and espionage
			Investigate potential threats to national security and allegations of disloyalty among federal employees
			Arrest alleged spies
			Investigate civil rights violations, racketeering, and gambling
			Investigate the assassination of a president
			Investigate individuals and organizations who threatened terrorism
1973–1979	Federal Bureau of Investigation	> 19,000 (including approximately 8,000 special agents)	Conduct foreign counterintelligence
			Investigate organized crime and white-collar crime
1979–2001	Federal Bureau of Investigation	> 23,000 (including 9,663 special agents)	Conduct foreign counterintelligence
			Investigate organized crime and white-collar crime
			Increase counterterrorism efforts
			Conduct drug investigations
			Investigate violent crime
2001–present	Federal Bureau of Investigation	> 28,000 (including > 12,000 special agents)	Prevent terrorist attacks
			Counter foreign intelligence operations against the United States
			Protect against cyber-based attacks and high-technology crimes

Source: FBI History. Available: http://www.fbi.gov/fbihistory.htm.

its own division within the FBI in 1942. Located in the J. Edgar Hoover building in Washington, D.C., the FBI Laboratory provides forensic examinations, technical support, expert witness testimony, and training to federal, state, and local law enforcement agencies. Laboratory services are provided in more than a dozen different areas of forensic science.[2] One of those areas is Computer Analysis and Response.

The FBI established the Computer Analysis and Response Team (CART) in 1984 to retrieve evidence from computers. It became fully operational in 1991. CART's mission is to provide digital forensics and technical capabilities, services, and support to the FBI, intelligence organizations, and other law enforcement agencies.[3] CART field examiners, all volunteers, are either Special Agents or Computer Specialists. The current staff of approximately 250 CART examiners are located at the FBI Laboratory and in the fifty-six FBI field offices throughout the United States. One of those field offices is located in New Haven, Connecticut.

FBI New Haven Field Office

The FBI's existence in Connecticut began in 1921, when one special agent from the Bureau of Investigation was assigned to the capital city of Hartford.[4] As the federal agency grew, so did the Connecticut field office. In 1941, the office moved to New Haven and over the next several decades, it moved to various locations in the downtown area. In February 2000, the New Haven field office moved to its current location at 600 State Street.[5]

The New Haven field office is the headquarters for FBI operations in Connecticut. Together with the two resident agencies located in Bridgeport and Meriden, there are more than 100 special agents and seventy-five professional support employees assigned to Connecticut. Each special agent is assigned to a squad that is responsible for a particular crime problem or investigative program (e.g., Counterterrorism, Counterintelligence, Computer Crime, Violent Crime, Drugs/Organized Crime,

Civil Rights). Professional support employees are assigned to squads, program managers, or other specialized units.[4]

The New Haven field office is home to the Connecticut Computer Crimes Task Force (CCCTF), a multi-agency task force established in March 2003 to investigate Internet crimes throughout Connecticut. These crimes include computer intrusion (state- or terrorist-sponsored and criminal), intellectual property theft, on-line crimes against children, Internet fraud, and identity theft.[6] The CCCTF is composed of agents from the FBI, the U.S. Postal Inspection Service, the Connecticut State Police, the Connecticut Chief State's Attorney's Office, the Defense Criminal Investigative Service, the Criminal Investigation Division of the Internal Revenue Service, the U.S. Secret Service, and detectives from area police departments.[7] Among the specialized functions based in the New Haven field office are the Crisis Negotiation Team, the Evidence Response Team, Special Weapons and Tactics, and CART.[5]

The following computer crime case was investigated by a Special Agent/CART field examiner in the FBI New Haven field office. The victim company is a Connecticut e-commerce company. Its name has been changed to BoatingCT.com to protect its identity. Specific customer names and their credit card numbers also have been changed, for the same reason. All other details are factual.

Computer Intrusion at BoatingCT.com

BoatingCT.com is a small business in Connecticut that specializes in the on-line sale of marine products. On April 24, 2001, the company began to receive e-mails from several of their customers. They were inquiring about the e-mail confirmations they had received shortly after they ordered products through the company's Web site. These e-mail messages, which contained the customer's on-line order number, the last four digits of the customer's credit card number, and the card's expiration date, requested the customer's credit card verification number and/or bank account information. BoatingCT.com had not sent these e-mail messages to their customers. The company contacted the FBI New Haven field office for investigative assistance, and at the FBI's request, it provided a copy of several e-mails received by its customers, along with its Web server logs. Figure 6-1 shows the text of an e-mail message received by a customer. Figure 6-2 shows the e-mail header information.

FBI Analysis

The e-mail header information shown in Figure 6-2 provided some important information (see Appendix A). Although the message appeared to be sent from orders@boatingct.com—the victim company's legitimate e-mail

---

Dear Mr. or Mrs. D,

We apologize for any inconvenience this may cause you, but our system has flagged your order most likely due to an unauthorized credit card transaction.

Ordernum: WEB11369

Visa: XXXX-XXXX-XXXX-1234

Exp: 09/02

In order for your items to be shipped we first need some verification. For our safety and security, BoatingCT requires that you respond back with your card's verification number, if one is available. The verification number is a 3-digit number printed on the back of your card. It appears after and to the right of your card number.

The second method is bank account verification in case fraudulent credit card information was provided. We require the routing number, which is located at the bottom of your check in between the |: and |: symbols, as well as the account number which comes before the ||' symbols. Exact location and number of digits varies between banks.

All information is private and confidential. Again, we apologize for any inconvenience and hope you continue to shop with us in the future.

FIGURE 6-1 Text of e-mail message sent to BoatingCT.com customer.

Source: Special Agent/CART field examiner, FBI New Haven Field Office, January 21, 2005.

Received: from ntmail1n.interaccess.com ([207.70.121.238])
        by gas-fs1.interaccess.com with SMTP (Microsoft Exchange
        Internet Mail Service

Version 5.5.2650.21)
        id JAYAG6ZX; Tue, 24 Apr 2001 03:04:45 -0500

Received: from janus.hosting4u.net ([209.15.2.37])
        by ntmail1n.interaccess.com (Post.Office MTA v3.5.3 release 223
        ID# 0-52801U100L2S100V35) with SMTP id com for
        <dand@abc.com>;
        Tue, 24 Apr 2001 03:16:06 -0500

Received: (qmail 8371 invoked from network); 24 Apr 2001 08:00:26 -0000

Received: from scorpius.hosting4u.net (209.15.2.32)
        by mail-gate.hosting4u.net with SMTP; 24 Apr 2001 08:00:26 -0000

To: dand@abc.com

From: orders@boatingct.com

Date:

Subject: Order Verification

Reply-To: boatingct@hotmail.com

FIGURE 6-2 E-mail header.

Source: Special Agent/CART field examiner, FBI New Haven Field Office, January 21, 2005.

address—the Reply-To address (boatingct@hotmail.com) was not the same. This indicated that the individual sending the e-mail confirmations to the company's customers was using a Hotmail account to obtain additional financial data from those customers. In addition, the presence of "hosting4u.net" in the Received headers indicated that the e-mail had passed through a Web hosting site. The CART field examiner used the ARIN site (http://www.arin.net/whois/) to determine that the owner of the IP addresses for hosting4u.net was CommuniTechnet. The system adminis-trator of CommuniTechnet was interviewed. During the interview, it was disclosed that CommuniTechnet hosted a site called Haxors.com, an e-mail spoofing site that could be used to hide an e-mail sender's identity.

A court order was issued to Hotmail.com, requiring them to preserve the subscriber information, billing information, logs, and e-mail related to boatingct@hotmail.com. The information provided by Hotmail showed that the boatingct@hotmail.com e-mail address had been registered to an individual named Jason Smith from Los Angeles, California, using IP address 210.120.192.30 (Figure 6-3). Searching the APNIC WHOIS database (http://www.apnic.net), the CART field examiner found that the owner of this IP address was BORANet, an Internet leased-line service located in Seoul, Korea. Hotmail's records showed that the boatingct@hotmail.com address had been set up from a computer in Seoul, and the account also had been checked from a computer in Seoul. The FBI New Haven field office contacted the Legat (FBI foreign liaison office) in Seoul, Korea, to obtain BORANet's Web logs.

Meanwhile, the CART field examiner began to search the web logs from BoatingCT.com for entries with specific reference to BORANet or its IP address. Figure 6-4 shows one of those entries, which contains the

Login:	boatingct@hotmail.com
First Name:	Jason
Last Name:	Smith
State:	California
Zip:	90210
Country:	US
Timezone:	America/Los_Angeles
Registered from IP:	210.120.192.30
Date registered:	Mon Apr 23 20:54:21 2001
Reply To Address:	Not available
Init Locale:	EN_US

FIGURE 6-3 Information from Hotmail.com regarding the boatingct@hotmail.com account.

Source: Special Agent/CART field examiner, FBI New Haven Field Office, January 21, 2005.

cache13.bora.net - - [23/Apr/2001:02:03:49 -0400] "GET /cgi-
bin/Web_store/web_store.cgi?page=../../../../../../../../home1/boatingct/cgi-
bin/Web_store/Admin_files/order.log%00.html HTTP/1.0" 200 85432 "-"
"Mozilla/4.0 (compatible; MSIE 5.5; Windows NT 5.0)"

FIGURE 6-4 **Suspicious entry in BoatingCT.com Web logs.**
Source: Special Agent/CART field examiner, FBI New Haven Field Office, January
21, 2005.

suspicious string "../../../../../../../../". The UNIX grep command was
used to search for this string in BoatingCT.com's Web logs and to
extract all log entries containing this string. Figure 6-5, which shows
some of the results from this search, contained entries from Ohio
(neo.rr.com), Turkey (ixir.net), and Korea (bora.net). A complete
analysis of the filtered Web logs showed that IPs from around the world
had accessed the order.log file at BoatingCT.com, using the string,
"../../../../../../../../".

The CART field examiner did an on-line search for the significance
of this string and found a full explanation at the SecuriTeam site
(http://www.securiteam.com/exploits/6W00L0A03C.html). In an alert
posted on October 12, 2000, SecuriTeam identified a directory traversal
vulnerability in WebStore version 1.0, a shopping cart software product
produced by eXtropia. A *directory traversal vulnerability* allows user
access to a restricted Web server file (e.g., a daily order file) that resides
outside of the Web server's root directory. The root directory should
prevent users from accessing files that reside outside of the root directory, while allowing user access to certain files that are stored in the root
directory and its subdirectories. Directory traversal vulnerabilities can
exist in a commercial Web server (e.g., Microsoft's Internet Information
Server) or in the application code that is executed on the Web server
(e.g., a company's shopping cart software).[8]

In this case, the vulnerability existed in BoatingCT.com's shopping cart
software, WebStore version 1.0. Figure 6-5 shows the exploitation of this

dhcp024.166.101.142.neo.rr.com - - [19/Apr/2001:14:49:46 -0400] "GET /cgi-bin/Web_store/web_store.cgi?page=../../../../../../../../ home1/boatingct/cgi-bin/Web_store/Admin_files/ order.log%00.html HTTP/1.1" 200 22194 "-" "Mozilla/4.0 (compatible; MSIE 5.5; Windows NT 5.0)"

north.ixir.net - - [19/Apr/2001:14:50:04 -0400] "GET /cgi-bin/Web_store/web_store.cgi?page=../../../../../../../../home1/boatingct/cgi-bin/Web_store/Admin_files/order.log%00.html HTTP/1.1" 200 22083 "-" "Mozilla/4.0 (compatible; MSIE 5.5; Windows NT 5.0)"

dhcp024.166.101.142.neo.rr.com - - [20/Apr/2001:02:46:25 -0400] "GET /cgi-bin/Web_store/web_store.cgi?page=../../../../../../../../ home1/boatingct/cgi-bin/Web_store/Admin_files/ order.log%00.html HTTP/1.1" 200 45712 "-" "Mozilla/4.0 (compatible; MSIE 5.5; Windows NT 5.0)"

north.ixir.net - - [20/Apr/2001:17:56:48 -0400] "GET /cgi-bin/Web_store/web_store.cgi?page=../../../../../../../../home1/boatingct/cgi-bin/Web_store/Admin_files/order.log%00.html HTTP/1.1" 200 29409 "-" "Mozilla/4.0 (compatible; MSIE 5.5; Windows NT 5.0)"

north.ixir.net - - [21/Apr/2001:03:07:34 -0400] "GET /cgi-bin/Web_store/web_store.cgi?page=../../../../../../../../home1/boatingct/cgi-bin/Web_store/Admin_files/order.log%00.html HTTP/1.1" 200 17546 "-" "Mozilla/4.0 (compatible; MSIE 5.5; Windows NT 5.0)"

dhcp024.166.101.142.neo.rr.com - - [22/Apr/2001:21:28:40 -0400] "GET /cgi-bin/Web_store/web_store.cgi?page=../../../../../../../../ home1/boatingct/cgi-bin/Web_store/Admin_files/ order.log%00.html HTTP/1.1" 200 79650 "-" "Mozilla/4.0 (compatible; MSIE 5.5; Windows NT 5.0)"

cache13.bora.net - - [23/Apr/2001:02:03:49 -0400] "GET /cgi-bin/Web_store/web_store.cgi?page=../../../../../../../../home1/boatingct/cgi-bin/Web_store/Admin_files/order.log%00.html HTTP/1.0" 200 85432 "-" "Mozilla/4.0 (compatible; MSIE 5.5; Windows NT 5.0)"

dhcp065.025.042.047.neo.rr.com - - [08/May/2001:13:54:47 -0400] "GET /cgi-bin/Web_store/web_store.cgi?page=../../../../../../../../ home1/boatingct/cgi-bin/Web_store/Admin_files/ order.log%00.html HTTP/1.1" 200 31 "-" "Mozilla/4.0 (compatible; MSIE 5.5; Windows NT 5.0)"

FIGURE 6-5 Filtered Web logs from BoatingCT.com.

Source: Special Agent/CART field examiner, FBI New Haven Field Office, January 21, 2005.

directory traversal vulnerability. The GET command allowed users to open the order.log file (home1/boatingct/cgi-bin/Web_store/Admin_files/order.log) and copy the file from BoatingCT.com's machine to their own machines. Intruders from around the world had gained unauthorized access to BoatingCT.com's daily order file, and to its customer order and credit card information. BoatingCT.com was informed of its software problem by the FBI. The company upgraded its shopping cart software to the latest version of WebStore (version 2.0), which was immune to this vulnerability. This patch had been available since October 2000, six months before the company's customers began to receive the suspicious e-mail confirmation messages requesting their credit card verification numbers and bank account information.

The CART field examiner's focus remained on identifying the sender of these suspicious e-mail messages, because this was the reason that BoatingCT.com had contacted the FBI New Haven field office. A further analysis of the log files provided by Hotmail revealed two particularly interesting IP addresses: 130.101.111.15 and 24.142.102.151. Using the ARIN site, the CART field examiner found that 130.101.111.15 was registered to the University of Akron. 24.142.102.151 turned out to be a free public proxy server located in Livermore, California, owned by Equinix.[9] Logs were requested from the Computer Center at the University of Akron, but none were available.

The CART field examiner found several entries in the Hotmail logs and the BoatingCT.com logs in which the WebStore directory traversal vulnerability had been exploited from an originating IP address of 24.142.102.151. The system administrator of this proxy server in California was contacted. The system administrator acknowledged that the server had little security, but offered to search their Web logs (using the UNIX grep command) for the strings "boatingct.com" and "order.log". Examples of the filtered log entries from the proxy server are shown in Figure 6-6. The first entry identifies the originating IP address of 24.166.101.142 executing the directory traversal exploit on

24.166.101.142-Apr-29:988598199 16389 24.166.101.142 TCP_MISS/200
105280 GET http://www.boatingct.com/cgi-
bin/Web_store/web_store.cgi?page=../../../../../../../../home1/boatingct/cgi-
bin/Web_store/Admin_files/order.log%00.html -
DIRECT/www.boatingct.com text/html

24.166.101.142-Apr-24:988181453 384 24.166.101.142
TCP_CLIENT_REFRESH/200 916 POST http://www.haxors.com/proto-
cell/cgi-bin/spoofer.cgi - DIRECT/www.haxors.com text/html

24.166.101.142-Apr-24:988180258 329 24.166.101.142 TCP_MISS/200
11317 GET http://lc1.law13.hotmail.passport.com/cgi-bin/login -
DIRECT/lc1.law13.hotmail.passport.com text/html

FIGURE 6-6 Sample filtered Web logs from the California Proxy Server (24.142.102.151).

Source: Special Agent/CART field examiner, FBI New Haven Field Office, January 21, 2005.

the order.log file on the BoatingCT.com Web site. The second entry shows this IP address (24.166.101.142) sending spoofed e-mail from the Haxors.com site. The third entry shows the same IP address accessing Hotmail.

This IP address (24.166.101.142), which appeared in dozens of the filtered log entries from the California proxy server, also appeared several times in BoatingCT.com's filtered Web logs, executing the directory traversal exploit (see Figure 6-5). The CART field examiner used the ARIN site to determine that this IP address was registered to Road Runner in Herndon, Virginia.

A further analysis of BoatingCT.com's filtered Web logs showed IP address 65.25.42.47 also executed the directory traversal exploit (see Figure 6-5). This IP address also was found to be registered to Road Runner in Herndon, Virginia. A court order was issued to the owner of Road Runner (Time Warner Cable), requiring them to preserve the subscriber information, billing information, logs, and e-mail related to IP addresses 24.166.101.142 and 65.25.42.47. The information provided by

Time Warner Cable indicated that the subscriber to the Road Runner IP addresses was a student who lived in a fraternity house at the University of Akron. (This was an interesting corroboration of a previous analysis of the log files provided by Hotmail, which revealed that the boatingct@hotmail.com account had been checked from a University of Akron computer.)

Seizing the Evidence and Performing Forensic Analysis

A search warrant was prepared in Connecticut and forwarded to the FBI Computer Crimes Task Force in Akron, Ohio. When the search warrant was executed at the fraternity house, the search team realized that there were a number of rooms with locked doors. To identify the suspect's room, the FBI agents used a ladder to look into the individual windows from outside of the building. The correct room was located when one of the residents opened his window.

During his interview, the student initially denied any wrongdoing, then admitted that he had hacked into BoatingCT.com's Web site and had taken customer order information, including their credit card numbers. He also admitted using proxy servers in other countries to cover his tracks. When the search team seized the student's computer system, they noticed that many of the cables were disconnected. He said that he was cleaning his computer, then confessed that when he heard the agents outside, he knew why they were there. He deleted the credit card information, then tried to destroy the master drive and hide it in the ceiling. Figure 6-7 shows the hard drive that was removed from the ceiling. The seized computer system was sent to the FBI New Haven field office for forensic analysis.

The computer system had two hard drives. The master drive, which had been partially destroyed, was sent to an outside vendor for data recovery. The vendor's efforts were unsuccessful. The FBI New Haven CART field examiners imaged the slave drive and used ILook[10] to ana-

FIGURE 6-7 Remains of the student's master drive.

Source: Special Agent/CART field examiner, FBI New Haven Field Office, January 21, 2005.

lyze its contents. Among the tests that were conducted using ILook was a search for the keywords "boatingct" and "boatingct.com", which was conducted on the free space and the slack space of the imaged hard drive. Data related to the intrusion at BoatingCT.com were recovered from the free space on the imaged hard drive. Samples of the recovered data are shown in Figures 6-8 through 6-11. Evidence that he had tried to sell the stolen customer credit cards also was retrieved from the imaged drive. Figures 6-12 and 6-13 show e-mails sent by the student (using the e-mail address daspang24@yahoo.com) for the purpose of selling the stolen cards.

Arrest and Sentencing

On June 13, 2002, the University of Akron student entered a guilty plea to one count of Title 18 US Code 1030 a(4) ("Fraud and related activity in connection with computers"). In so doing, he admitted to "knowingly and with the intent to defraud, access a protected computer, without

ORDERNUM: WEB11712
DATE: 04/30/01 19:20

Billing - First Name   = Beverly
Billing - Last Name   = C
Billing - Attention=
Billing - Address 1   = 3 Land Point Rd.
Billing - Address 2   =
Billing—City   = Lotburg
Billing - State   = VA
Billing - ZIP   = 22333

Payment - Method   = American Express
Payment - Card Name   = Beverly A. C
Card Number   = 1234 5678 1234 5678
Payment - Card Exp   = 11/02

Items Ordered:

Catalog Item Number: 5033
Model Number: BVret
Description: 3/4" fitting
Quantity: 2
Net Each: 58.79

FIGURE 6-8 One of the BoatingCT.com customer order records retrieved from the student's computer.

Source: Special Agent/CART field examiner, FBI New Haven Field Office, January 21, 2005.

authorization" to obtain credit card information. He also admitted to preparing and sending fraudulent e-mail messages to the company's customers to obtain additional financial information, and to using some of the credit card and financial information for his own personal gain. His arraignment took place in the United States District Court, District of Connecticut, in downtown New Haven. A loss figure of $335,000 was stipulated, determined on the basis of the number of credit cards he stole (670) multiplied by the minimum implied loss per credit card ($500). He

Dear Mr. or Mrs. G,

We apologize for any inconvenience this may cause you, but our system has flagged your order most likely due to an unauthorized credit card transaction.

Ordernum: WEB11341
Visa: XXXX-XXXX-XXXX-0421
Exp: 11/02

In order for your items to be shipped we first need some verification. For our safety and security, BoatingCT requires that you respond back with your card's verification number, if one is available. The verification number is a 3-digit number printed on the back of your card. It appears after and to the right of your card number.

The second method is bank account verification in case fraudulent credit card information was provided. We require the routing number, which is located at the bottom of your check in between the I: and I: symbols, as well as the account number which comes before the II' symbols. Exact location and number of digits varies between banks.

All information is private and confidential. Again, we apologize for any inconvenience and hope you continue to shop with us in the future.

FIGURE 6-9 Text of e-mail message sent to a BoatingCT.com customer retrieved from the student's computer.

Source: Special Agent/CART field examiner, FBI New Haven Field Office, January 21, 2005.

was sentenced to twelve months in prison and required to pay $20,000 in restitution to BoatingCT.com. On October 22, 2003, he was released from prison after serving approximately six months of his sentence. The case was officially closed on February 23, 2004.

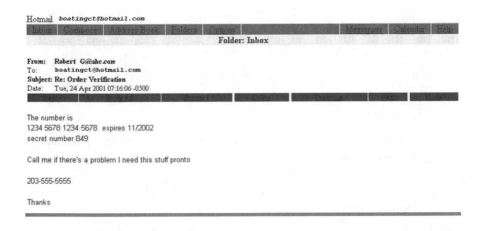

FIGURE 6-10 BoatingCT.com customer e-mail responses retrieved from the student's computer.

Source: Special Agent/CART field examiner, FBI New Haven Field Office, January 21, 2005.

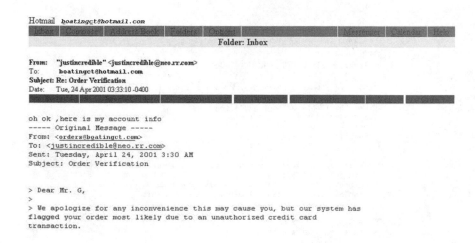

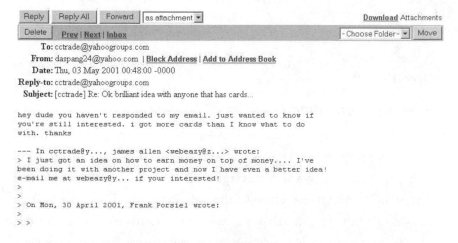

FIGURE 6-11 The student's test message and response to himself retrieved from his computer.

Source: Special Agent/CART field examiner, FBI New Haven Field Office, January 21, 2005.

FIGURE 6-12 The student's e-mail to sell stolen customer credit cards retrieved from his computer.

Source: Special Agent/CART field examiner, FBI New Haven Field Office, January 21, 2005.

From: "Joka" <jnona@EUnet.yu> | Block Address | Add to Address Book
   To: "David Spang" <daspang24@yahoo.com>
Subject: Re: links
   Date: Sat, 5 May 2001 04:40:51 +0200

```
First two numbers are hidden, please check.
----- Original Message -----
From: "David Spang" <daspang24@yahoo.com>
To: "Joka" <jnona@EUnet.yu>
Sent: Saturday, May 05, 2001 3:04 AM
Subject: Re: links


> here's a few cards. I don't know the limit on them
> mind you, so I probably wouldn't try to order maybe
> more than $200 on them. unless you have some way to
> find out the balance or limit on them. use this
> address to send the money to:
>
> Treasurer
> 380 E. Buchtel Ave.
> Akron, OH 44304
> USA
>
> ORDERNUM: WEB11860 DATE: 05/03/01 08:39
> ----------------------------------------
> -------------------------------------------------
```

FIGURE 6-13 The student's e-mail to sell stolen customer credit cards retrieved from his computer. The Akron, Ohio, address given in his e-mail is the address of his fraternity house.

Source: Special Agent/CART field examiner, FBI New Haven Field Office, January 21, 2005.

Appendix A

Gathering Information From the E-mail Header

When an e-mail message is sent, it goes from the sender's system to a mail server program, also known as a message transfer agent. The mail server program receives the message from the sender's message user agent, which is the name given to the software that allows the user to access and manage e-mail (e.g., Microsoft Outlook, Lotus Notes, Eudora). The mail server program (e.g., Microsoft Exchange Server, UNIX sendmail), puts its Internet Protocol (IP) address and the current date and time in a Received header at the top of the e-mail message. It then passes the message to the next mail server program on a different computer. Each mail server program that handles the message puts its own Received header at the top before the message is transferred. The message is passed from one system to another, with each mail server program adding its own Received header to the top of the message, until the message reaches its correct destination. The route that the e-mail traveled from the sender's system to the final destination can be tracked by reading the Received headers sequentially, from bottom to top.

Because mail server programs exchange messages using Simple Mail Transfer Protocol (SMTP), it is possible for an individual to instruct the mail server program directly by using Telnet. Forged Received headers can be inserted into an e-mail message by using SMTP's Data command; however, these fictitious headers can be detected. The Data command inserts these headers within the body of the message; a suspicious placement because legitimate headers are placed above the message. Also, forged Received headers often have date and time stamps that are inconsistent with those in the nonforged Received headers.

A sender's IP address can be hidden by sending e-mail through a Web proxy service to an SMTP server. If a Web proxy server is used, the header contains the IP address of the proxy server. The IP addresses listed in the headers can be used to trace back to the originating computer. The process begins by identifying the Internet Service Provider (ISP) responsible for the IP address in question. The ISP can be identified through a WHOIS site. A number of WHOIS sites exist, although the following three sites are considered definitive sources:

- *ARIN*—American Registry for Internet Numbers (Western Hemisphere): http://www.arin.net/whois/.
- *APNIC*—Asia Pacific Network Information Centre (Asia-Pacific): http://www.apnic.net.
- *RIPE NCC*—Réseaux IP Européens Network Coordination Center (Europe): http://www.ripe.net.

Once the ISP has been identified, it can be contacted to identify the owner of the computer in question.

Endnotes

1. "The FBI Strategic Plan, 2004–2009." Available: http://www.fbi.gov/ publications/strategicplan/stategicplantext.htm.
2. "FBI Laboratory Services." Available: http://www.fbi.gov/hq/ lab/org/labchart.htm.
3. Kenneth J. Morrison, "The Impact of Digital Forensics on FBI Criminal Investigations," presented at the Connecticut chapter of the Information Systems Security Association, November 9, 2004.
4. "FBI New Haven, Connecticut Division—About Us." Available: http://newhaven.fbi.gov/about_us.htm.
5. "FBI New Haven, Connecticut Division—New Haven Division." Available: http://newhaven.fbi.gov/new_haven.htm.
6. Personal communication with a Supervisory Special Agent, FBI New Haven, January 22, 2005.
7. FBI National Press Office, Washington, D.C., June 30, 2004, "Connecticut Computer Crimes Task Force." Available: http://www.fbi.gov/ pressrel04/compcrimes063004.htm.
8. Imperva Application Defense Center, "Directory Traversal." Available: http://www.imperva.com/application_defense_center/glossary/directory_traversal.html.
9. At the time of this writing, 24.142.102.151 is registered to Loral CyberStar in Rockville, Maryland. In 2002, Loral CyberStar established satellite IP service operations in Equinix's Internet Business Exchange centers. See Equinix Press Release, "Loral CyberStar Teams with Equinix to Enhance Delivery of Satellite IP Network Services to Global Enterprises," February 20, 2002. Available: http://www.equinix.com/press/press/2002/02_20_02.htm.

10. ILook (http://www.Ilook-forensics.org) is one of several computer forensic software tools used by the FBI. Others include FTK or Forensic Toolkit (http://www.accessdata.com/Product04_Overview.htm), EnCase (http://www.encase.com/), WinHex (http://www.x-ways.com/winhex/index-m.html), and Message Digest 5 or MD5 (http://theory.lcs.mit.edu/~rivest/rfc1321.txt).

Case Study Questions

1. What should the Connecticut company have done to prevent the computer intrusion described in this case? What should it have done to detect this computer intrusion?

2. What security controls should be implemented by any organization to prevent, detect, and recover from a computer intrusion?

3. Why would someone want to use a forged e-mail address? Explain how this worked to the intruder's advantage in this case.

4. Numerous entries similar to the following were found in Boating CT.com's Web logs. What does this entry mean?
   spider-we084.proxy.aol.com - - [23/Apr/2001:02:04:14 -0400] "GET / cgi-bin/Web_store/web_store.cgi?keywords=803103&frames=yes& store=yes HTTP/1.0" 200 2164 "http://www.boatingct.com/" "Mozilla/ 4.0 (compatible; MSIE 5.5; AOL 6.0; Windows 98; Win 9x 4.90)"

5. What was the importance of having court orders immediately issued to Hotmail.com and Time Warner Cable?

6. When the FBI New Haven field office requested the log files from the University of Akron, none were available. Do you think it is typical for universities not to retain log files? What is the impact of this on the security of university computing environments?

7. The FBI New Haven CART field examiners imaged the hard drive and worked off of that. They did not use the original drive or the original evidence. Why?

8. When the Web logs from BoatingCT.com were analyzed, the CART field examiner discovered that intruders from around the world had gained unauthorized access to the company's daily order file. The company was informed of this, but the CART field examiner's focus remained on identifying the sender of the suspicious e-mails to BoatingCT.com's customers, the reason given for the FBI's involvement in this case. What other reasons might the FBI have had for not pursuing these other intruders?

9. The computer intruder described in this case was a U.S. citizen who resided in Ohio. What would the FBI have done if he were a non-U.S. citizen who resided in a foreign country?

10. What types of Internet-related crimes should be reported to the FBI? At what point should a computer crime be reported to law enforcement?

KEY TERMS

American Registry for Internet Numbers (ARIN): Nonprofit organization that registers and administers IP addresses for North America. See http://www.arin.net/whois/.

Asia Pacific Network Information Centre (APNIC): Nonprofit organization that registers and administers IP addresses for the Asia-Pacific region. See http://www.apnic.net.

Directory Traversal Vulnerability: An exploit that allows a user to take advantage of a particular software flaw to gain unauthorized access to restricted files that reside outside of the Web server's root directory.

E-mail Spoofing: Forging an e-mail header so that the message appears to have come from someone or somewhere other than the original source.

EnCase: Computer forensic software from Guidance Software used by commercial organizations, law enforcement, and government agencies. See http://www.encase.com.

Free Space: Empty space on a hard disk.

Forensic Toolkit (FTK): Computer forensic software from AccessData used by law enforcement and corporate security professionals. See http://www.accessdata.com/Product04_Overview.htm.

GET: A file transfer protocol (FTP) command used to download files.

Global-Regular-Expression-Print (GREP): A UNIX command that allows a user to search for a particular string and output all lines that contain that string.

ILook: Computer forensic software developed by Perlustro LP and the Internal Revenue Service, Criminal Investigation Division, Electronic Crimes Program. It is used by law enforcement and government agencies, and is not available commercially. See http://www.Ilook-forensics.org/.

Image (of a drive): An exact copy of the hard drive.

Internet Protocol Address (IP address): A 32-bit numeric address for a computer, written as a dotted quad: four numbers separated by periods, with each number ranging from 0 to 255.

Internet Service Provider (ISP): Company that provides access to the Internet.

Mail Server Program: See Message Transfer Agent.

Master Drive: Main drive. In general, the operating system boots from the master drive.

Message Digest 5 (MD5): Algorithm created by Ronald Rivest in 1991 as a way to verify data integrity. The algorithm uses a one-way hash function to convert a variable-length message into a 128-bit string of digits. This output string is called a *message digest*. Each message has a unique message digest. Any change to the message results in a different message digest. In computer forensics, the MD5 value of a file is computed before data collection and again after data collection. If the MD5 values match, the files are believed to be identical. A full explanation can be found at http://theory.lcs.mit.edu/~rivest/rfc1321.txt.

Message Transfer Agent (MTA): Program responsible for routing e-mail messages between computers.

Message User Agent (MUA): E-mail software that provides the interface between the user and the message transfer agent.

Proxy Server: Device that forwards requests between a Web browser and the requested Web site.

Réseaux IP Européens Network Coordination Center (RIPE NCC): Nonprofit organization that registers and administers IP addresses for Europe. See http://www.ripe.net.

Simple Mail Transfer Protocol (SMTP): Recognized format for sending e-mails between servers on the Internet.

Slack Space: Space on the hard disk between the end of a file and the end of the cluster that the file occupies.

Slave Drive: Secondary drive.

Telnet: Terminal emulation program that allows remote access to computers on the Internet.

Web Host: Company that leases server space and Web services to those who want an Internet presence but do not want to maintain their own servers.

WHOIS: Internet program that returns information about an IP address or a domain name.

WinHex: Universal hexadecimal editor from X-Ways Software Technology AG. Used for computer forensics and data recovery. See http://www.x-ways.net/winhex/index-m.html.

AETNA:
DEVELOPING AND IMPLEMENTING A SUCCESSFUL INFORMATION SECURITY AWARENESS PROGRAM

The process of developing and implementing a successful internal security awareness program is complicated and difficult. The results for most organizations are ineffective programs that do not improve information security practices. Aetna succeeded in establishing a cost-effective program that measurably improves its users' security behaviors. Its security awareness program is based on realistic goals, ties security with the business environment, reflects the corporate culture, uses multiple delivery mechanisms to reinforce the security message, ensures that all users are exposed to information security training, provides the ability to measure the knowledge being transferred, and receives continued support from senior-level managers and executives.

This case study describes the information security awareness program at Aetna. Emphasis is placed on the Information Security (InfoSec) exam, the most significant element of the employee security awareness program. To place this program in context, the case study begins with an overview of Aetna, its history, and its information security program organization.

Aetna—The Company

Aetna is one of the United States' leading providers of health care, dental, pharmacy, group life, disability, and long-term care insurance and employee benefits. The company's 2004 reported net income was $2.2 billion on total revenue of $19.9 billion. As of December 30, 2004, the company had approximately 27,000 employees, 13.7 million medical members, 11.9 million dental members, 8.4 million pharmacy members, and 13.5 million group insurance customers. It also had a nationwide provider network of more than 655,000 health care professionals, including over 390,000 primary care and specialty physicians and 3,937 hospitals.[1] The company has been listed on the New York Stock Exchange since 1968. It trades under the symbol AET.

History

The Hartford, Connecticut–based insurance company was started in 1853, when the Aetna Life Insurance Company was incorporated. By 1865, it was one of the largest life insurance companies in the nation, with annual income in excess of $1 million. It remained solely a life insurance company until 1891, when it issued its first accident insurance policy. In 1899, Aetna began to offer individual health insurance policies, although those policies initially were issued only to its life or accident insurance policy holders. By 1904, Aetna was the largest life insurance company in the world. During the next ten years, Aetna expanded into liability insurance (e.g., employers' liability insurance and workmen's compensation insurance), property and casualty insurance, and fidelity and surety coverage. The company added group life insurance policies in 1913, followed by group accident insurance policies

(1914), group disability insurance policies (1919), and group health insurance policies (1936).[2]

Beginning in the 1930s, Aetna insured a number of large-scale projects. In 1931, it bonded the construction of the Hoover Dam. The following year, it bonded the construction of the National Archives Building in Washington, D.C. It provided insurance coverage for the Manhattan Project in 1944, and that same year, it became the first insurance company to advertise on television. In 1949, Aetna bonded the construction of the United Nations headquarters in New York.[2]

Aetna expanded into the field of international insurance in 1960, when it acquired the Excelsior Life Insurance Company, a Canadian firm. By 1981, it had acquired interests in insurance companies in Australia, Chile, England, Hong Kong, Indonesia, Korea, Spain, and Taiwan.[2]

In 1990, the company stopped issuing individual health insurance policies, thereby ending a practice that had been in place for ninety-one years. Over the next decade, a number of strategic decisions were made that ultimately led to Aetna's transformation from a multiline insurance company to a company focused on health care and group benefits insurance. In 1996, Aetna sold its property and casualty operations and it purchased U.S. Healthcare. Over the next three years, it acquired the managed health care plans of New York Life Insurance Company and Prudential Insurance Company of America. By the time it sold its financial services and international businesses in 2000, Aetna had completed its transformation into one of the largest health care companies in the nation.[2]

Information Security

Prior to 1987, information security was the responsibility of three corporate-level entities. The Computer Security function established information systems security policy, the Information Systems function handled the computer center backup and disaster recovery planning, and the Facilities Risk Management group was responsible for other security, safety, and insurance activities.[3]

In March 1987, these three functions were consolidated to form a new corporate security/risk management group. This group was responsible for establishing corporate information security policy, overseeing disaster recovery and business continuity planning, addressing application design and security risks, and developing and implementing security awareness programs. However, each division maintained its own information processing operations and each had its own data security officer.[3]

In 1990, Janus Associates—an independent information technology (IT) security firm—was hired to assess Aetna's computer security, identify gaps, and make recommendations for strengthening the company's IT security. The security firm made three recommendations: centralize the security administration process in an enterprise-wide security administration function, centralize the policy making and high-level security functions within the Aetna Information Technology unit, and monitor activities based on established policies, practices, and procedures.[3] By the end of 1991, Aetna had reorganized into strategic business units,[2] and all of the business continuity and IT security functions had been merged within the Aetna Information Technology unit.[3]

In 1993, Aetna adopted a trusted systems approach to business continuity and IT security.[3] A number of information security policies, standards and procedures subsequently were issued[4]:

- The "End-to-End IT Security Strategy" was published in November 1993. It provided the general vision, direction, and high-level models associated with the company's security strategy.[3]
- In April 1994, "Aetna IT Security Standards" was published. This document identified the required information security controls to be used in the development, maintenance, and audit of all business and technology systems.[3]
- The "Procedure for Business Continuity Controls" was published in June 1994 in the "Corporate Controller's Accounting & Con-

trol Policies Manual." It defined business unit and employee responsibilities for ensuring continuous business operations and the protection of IT resources and information assets.[3]

▪ In July 1994, "Aetna Business Continuity Standards" was published. This was a composite of standards and best practices developed with input from other industry leaders and outside experts.[3]

▪ The "Business Continuity and IT Security Reference Guide" was published in November 1994. It provided business managers with general guidelines on how to protect IT resources and information assets, how to ensure continuity of critical business functions in the aftermath of a disruptive event, and how to fulfill their responsibilities for complying with the company's business continuity policy.[3]

Beginning in late 1994, the organizational placement of information security was realigned. The structure and responsibilities of the Aetna Information Technology unit were refocused, effectively transferring the responsibility for information security from this centralized corporate organization to the business units. This shift in responsibility was facilitated through the implementation of a Security Access Request System. This system—a front-end, automated access request, verification, and authorization process—allowed access administration to be moved from the Aetna Information Technology unit (where it had been performed since the 1991 consolidation) to the business IT areas.[3]

In February 1995, employee security awareness and education was moved from the Aetna Information Technology unit to the business units. Over the course of the next three years, there was little visible effort by the business units to promote the understanding of information security. Although the business units operated in compliance with the company's IT security policies, standards, and procedures, concerns started to surface regarding Aetna's ability to demonstrate due care.[3] In 1998, the company addressed these concerns by implementing a comprehensive information security awareness program under the auspices of the Information Security Policy and Practices (ISPP) group.

Information Security Program Organization

Aetna's information security awareness program is managed by the company's ISPP group. The five employees in this group are collectively responsible for all aspects of information security management, including[5]:

- developing and publicizing the company's security policies, standards, guidelines, and procedures;
- developing and maintaining Aetna's security portal (SecurNet);
- establishing the communication plan for the information security awareness program;
- handling all project management activities for the externally developed InfoSec exam;
- marketing the security awareness program throughout the enterprise;
- providing security training to all employees (e.g., general users, contract workers, application developers, managers, executives);
- coordinating with internal and external audits; and
- supporting all information security reviews and investigations.

Aetna's information security program organization is depicted in Figure 7-1. As shown in this diagram, the head of the Information Security Policy and Practices group reports to the Chief Information Officer (CIO) through Integrated User Services. The relatively high placement of the ISPP group within the organizational structure is a contributing factor to the success of the company's employee security awareness program.

The head of the ISPP group and the head of the Security Services group serve as co-chairs of the Information Security Committee (ISC). This committee helps to provide governance for the company's overall information security program, and it consists of decision-making managers from Legal, Audit, Disaster Recovery Planning Services, Business Continuity, Corporate Security and Compliance, as well as Business Security/Privacy Managers, and the HIPAA Privacy Project Management Office. The CIO chairs the IT Steering Committee, which consists of senior-level executives from the same areas as those represented

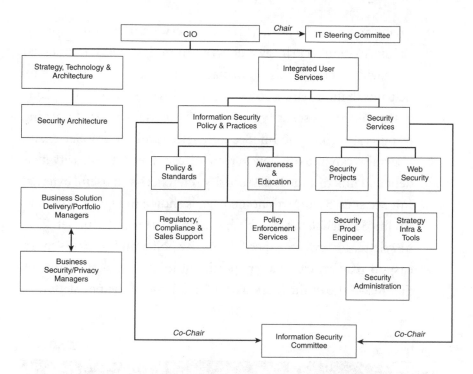

FIGURE 7-1 Enterprise Information Security Program Organization.

Source: Donna Richmond, "Tips, Tricks & Techniques of a Successful Security Awareness Program," presented at the InfraGard Connecticut Quarterly Meeting, February 2, 2005.

on the Information Security Committee and mirrors the ISC in purpose and function.

The Business Security/Privacy Managers role exists within each business unit to disseminate policies, monitor business information systems security, and investigate and resolve security incidents.[3]

Information Security Awareness Program

The goal of Aetna's program is to persuade all of its users to employ good security practices and behaviors. To achieve this goal, the ISPP group has delivered several mechanisms to convey and reinforce the importance of security[5]:

■ An intranet security portal, SecurNet, serves as the foundation for all information security awareness communications. It is designed to provide users with the information they need to be active participants in information security. From this site, users can read any of the company's security policies and access Web-based learning resources, such as the InfoSec newsletter and the InfoSec exam. Users also can find out how to recognize and report a security incident and link to additional security references and useful external InfoSec sites. SecurNet's home page is shown in Figure 7-2.

■ An InfoSec newsletter is published each quarter on SecurNet. Each newsletter focuses on a specific security policy and contains short, easy-to-read articles that are pertinent to the newsletter's theme. Figure 7-3 shows the first quarter 2005 issue of the newsletter.

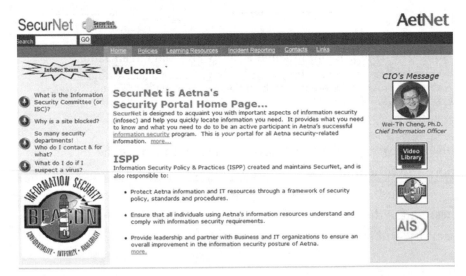

FIGURE 7-2 Home page of SecurNet, Aetna's intranet information security portal.

Source: Donna Richmond, "Tips, Tricks & Techniques of a Successful Security Awareness Program," presented at the InfraGard Connecticut quarterly meeting, February 2, 2005.

- Barrel pens with a security theme are distributed as promotional give aways. The side window of each pen displays one of six possible security messages when the pen is clicked.
- Brown bag lunches are held each quarter to discuss security topics of personal user interest. These topics (e.g., personal firewalls, virus protection) ultimately relate to the organization's need for good security practices.
- The ISPP group participates in the company's annual Customer Service Fair. The group uses this internal event to raise user awareness of security in general and ISPP's function in particular.
- Professional-looking posters that advertise the brown bag lunches and the Customer Service Fairs are developed in partnership with

FIGURE 7-3 First quarter 2005 issue of "The Beacon," Aetna's InfoSec newsletter.

Source: Donna Richmond, "Tips, Tricks & Techniques of a Successful Security Awareness Program," presented at the InfraGard Connecticut quarterly meeting, February 2, 2005.

Aetna's Advertising Design department and distributed throughout the organization.

■ An InfoSec exam provides security training and testing for all users on an annual basis.

Since its inception in 1999, Aetna's information security awareness program has received professional recognition. In 2000, the SANS Institute identified it as "the model" for other organizations to emulate. It also received the Information Security Program of the Year award in 2002 from the Computer Security Institute.[5] The program's champion is Donna Richmond, who is responsible for Security Awareness and Education in the Information Security Policy and Practices group.

InfoSec Exam—Overview

The key element of Aetna's security awareness program is its mandatory InfoSec exam. This Web-based exam, accessible through SecurNet, must be completed every year by all users, including managers. The InfoSec exam is updated annually to incorporate security topics that are relevant to Aetna's environment. The ISPP group determines the security topics, in consultation with subject matter experts and the ISC. The topics are based on business needs, current industry practices, and government regulations.

Each exam builds on the strengths of the previous exam and attempts to correct obvious weaknesses. When the first exam was implemented in 1999, it consisted of a series of learning topics (Table 7-1). These were followed by a separate twenty-question test. If the user did not correctly answer all of the questions, the user had to retake the entire exam.[5] The exam was perceived as draconian, and the following year it was redesigned to be more user friendly. The new design created better opportunities to successfully transfer knowledge.

Subsequent exams were divided into independent and interactive modules. Each module requires approximately ten minutes to complete and the entire exam can be finished in one hour or less. The modules

TABLE 7-1 1999 InfoSec Exam

LEARNING TOPIC	TITLE
1	Importance of Security and Confidentiality
2	Protecting Aetna Confidential Information
3	Restricting Use
4	Preventing Unauthorized Access
5	Maintaining a Stable Computing Environment

Source: E-mail communication with Donna Richmond, Security Advisor, Information Security Policy and Practices, Aetna, February 25, 2005.

can be completed at each user's convenience and they do not need to be finished all at once. Questions are incorporated within each module to reinforce the subject matter and to keep the users engaged. If the user enters two incorrect answers to a question, the correct answer is displayed along with a brief explanation. Aetna believes this to be the optimal model for transferring knowledge and improving its users' security behaviors.

Each exam has a different focus and each module addresses a different security topic. For example, the 2000 InfoSec exam focused on confidentiality. The 2001 and 2002 InfoSec exams emphasized different aspects of the Health Insurance Portability and Accountability Act (HIPAA). The 2003 and 2004 InfoSec exams were integrated within the company's Business Conduct and Integrity training program and they addressed various facets of information security. The modules for each of these InfoSec exams are shown in Tables 7-2 through 7-6.

In addition to the exam's redesign, improvements were made in the way it was targeted to employees. Role-based exams were introduced, enabling the security topics to be focused more directly toward different groups of users. For example, general users received Web-based training on important legislation relevant to the health care industry; application

TABLE 7-2 2000 InfoSec Exam

MODULE	TITLE
1	Appropriate Software Use
2	Hack Attacks and Hoaxes
3	Recovering Your Data
4	Proper Use of Company Resources
5	Protecting Confidential Information
6	Smart Security Practices

Source: E-mail communication with Donna Richmond, Security Advisor, Information Security Policy and Practices, Aetna, February 25, 2005.

developers received on-line training concerning appropriate checks for security throughout the systems development life cycle; management's on-line training reminded them of their role in controlling access based on need-to-know principles; and senior-level executives were given off-line, face-to-face presentations that focused on the legal costs associated with poor security.[6]

TABLE 7-3 2001 InfoSec Exam

MODULE	TITLE
1	HIPAA Administrative Simplification and Privacy
2	HIPAA Privacy
3	Security Is Good Business
4	InfoSec Incident Reporting
5	Electronic Communications

Source: E-mail communication with Donna Richmond, Security Advisor, Information Security Policy and Practices, Aetna, February 25, 2005.

TABLE 7-4 2002 InfoSec Exam

MODULE	TITLE
1	Information Security Policy and Practices
2	Internet Security and Malicious Code
3	People, Property, and Asset Protection
4	Contingency Planning
5	HIPAA Privacy Regulations
6	Privacy Policy and Procedures

Source: E-mail communication with Donna Richmond, Security Advisor, Information Security Policy and Practices, Aetna, February 25, 2005.

TABLE 7-5 2003 InfoSec Exam

MODULE	TITLE
1	Introduction
2	Regulatory Compliance
3	Privacy
4	Information Security
	Proper Use of Resources (Internet/E-mail)
	E-Mail Etiquette
	Workstation Security
	Passwords
	InfoSec Incidents
5	Integrity
6	Raising Concerns

Source: E-mail communication with Donna Richmond, Security Advisor, Information Security Policy and Practices, Aetna, February 25, 2005.

TABLE 7-6 2004 InfoSec Exam

MODULE	TITLE
1	Introduction
2	Regulatory Compliance
3	Privacy
4	Information Security
	Confidentiality
	InfoSec Incidents
	Physical Access
	Business Associate Contracts
	Device and Media Controls
	Integrity
	Workstation Security
	Passwords
	Availability
	Business Continuity
	Proper Use of Resources
5	Integrity
6	Ethics
7	Raising Concerns

Source: E-mail communication with Donna Richmond, Security Advisor, Information Security Policy and Practices, Aetna, February 25, 2005.

Additional improvements were made in the administration of the InfoSec exam. Specifically, monitoring tools were developed so that management could identify those employees who had not yet completed the annual exam for targeted follow-up. These tools also enabled the ISPP group to monitor the overall exam completion rate and to determine further communication plans.

InfoSec Exam—Design and Development

Team work is involved in the design and development of each InfoSec exam. The process begins with the establishment of a baseline for the target audience.[6] Tools for on-line user registration, status process, and compliance reporting are created by the Internal IT Development group in consultation with the ISPP group. On-line registration requires each user to read a condensed version of the company's Information Security Statement of Policy[4] and to electronically agree to comply with that policy[5] before the user can proceed with the exam.

The ISPP group also works with selected subject matter experts to ensure accurate exam content and terminology. Different subject matter experts are needed for each module of the exam. Each exam has several modules, and at least three subject matter experts provide input for each module.[6]

Actual development of the InfoSec exam is contracted to a local eLearning vendor. For an organization the size of Aetna, the ISPP group found that it was more economical to pay for custom development than to purchase a generic security exam. Off-the-shelf exams from security awareness solution providers were estimated to cost between $4 and $12 per user.[5] The cost of customized development was determined to be less than $2 per user[5] and allowed Aetna to capitalize on the availability of its subject matter experts and information security personnel. The ISPP group worked with Human Performance Technologies in Farmington, Connecticut, for the development of its initial InfoSec exams (1999 through 2002), and then with its spin-off firm, Peak Performers in West Hartford, Connecticut, for later versions of the exam. Each version of the exam requires the team leader, technical writer, graphics designer, and application programmer from the eLearning firm to develop the storyboard and code the exam modules. This process can take up to two months to complete.

Once the prototype is developed, it undergoes usability testing by the Human Factors Engineering group at Aetna. The purpose of usability testing is to ensure that the content of each module is acceptable to the users and that the exam is easy to navigate. The Usability Lab is located at Aetna's Hartford, Connecticut, headquarters. The ISPP group selects users to participate in the testing drawn from a variety of work groups at this same location. The users are chosen on the basis of their willingness to participate and their level of technological capability. Most of the eight to ten users who are selected have an entry-level understanding of computers and tend to be uncomfortable with Web-based applications.[6]

The Usability Lab is equipped with cameras that are focused on each user's face, keyboard, and monitor during testing.[6] After the test, which takes about an hour to complete, the recordings are reviewed. Careful attention is given to any changes in user facial expressions, particularly those that indicate frustration or uncertainty, along with the parts of the exam that prompted these changes.

Any necessary modifications to the modules are made by the eLearning vendor, and then the InfoSec exam application code is turned over to Aetna's Information Services group so that it can be embedded in the infrastructure. The application code is linked to the employee database so that each user's exam registration and completion activity can be monitored, and it is tested for quality assurance and stress performance before it becomes operational. Quality assurance testing is done to ensure that the code is compatible with user desktop configurations.[6] This testing is designed to troubleshoot interoperability problems and to reduce the number of individual calls for assistance when the users access the InfoSec exam through their desktop machines. Stress testing is done to ensure that the application code can function efficiently when a large volume of users simultaneously attempt to access it. When the testing is complete, the InfoSec exam is ready for enterprise implementation.

It takes approximately six months to design and develop each version of the InfoSec exam. After six months of an exam's operation, the process begins again to design and develop the next version.

Implementation

In an organization the size of Aetna, implementation of the InfoSec exam must be done in a phased manner. The first group to be notified is the HelpDesk/Desktop Support. Approximately one week before the InfoSec exam becomes operational, the ISPP group sends an e-mail to the HelpDesk/Desktop Support personnel, informing them that a new InfoSec exam is going to be implemented and forewarning them that there may be a potential increase in user calls for assistance.[6]

A few days after the HelpDesk/Desktop Support group is notified, an e-mail is sent to all managers.[6] The e-mail notifies them about the new InfoSec exam and reminds them of the purpose and importance of security awareness training.[6]

All employees are informed of the new InfoSec exam via e-mail from the ISPP group. The e-mails are sent a few days after management is notified, and they are distributed in increments so that not all of the users are informed at once. This avoids placing an undue burden on the infrastructure and the HelpDesk/Desktop Support group.[6]

New users receive a special e-mail notification, sent to them on the first day of their employment. The e-mail provides them with a link to the Web-based New Employee Orientation Program.[5] This program includes an overview of information security and a six-minute InfoSec Orientation streamed video. Both the overview and the video introduce the new users to the topic of information security and identify ways in which they can practice good security. The New Employee Orientation Program also includes a link to the InfoSec exam.[5] The exam must be completed within one month of hire and annually thereafter.

All employees must go through an on-line registration process before they are allowed to take any InfoSec exam. The process, which requires each employee to electronically agree to abide by the company's Information Security Statement of Policy,[4] creates an evidential record of user comprehension and compliance that is maintained by the company.[6]

When the InfoSec exam is finished, each employee can print out a certificate of completion.[5] The certificate is personalized and includes a customized information security message. Employees often display their certificates in their work areas, which serves to reinforce the importance of security throughout the organization.

Compliance

The ISPP group regularly analyzes the exam statistics throughout the testing period cycle. Status process and compliance reporting tools enable them to evaluate the completion progress according to individual employee, cost center and enterprise-wide groups.[5] Management can use an on-line data retrieval utility to keep track of their employees' overall exam completion rates and to identify those who have not completed the entire exam.

E-mail reminders occasionally have to be sent from the ISPP group to management, and from management to specific users. The ISPP group sends e-mails as needed to managers, reminding them to take the InfoSec exam and prompting them to monitor the progress of their employees' compliance. Management, in turn, sends e-mail reminders to those users who still need to complete the exam.

Aetna's comprehensive monitoring and communication plans have resulted in an impressive compliance rate: all of its users and managers have completed every InfoSec exam each year since 2000.

Endnotes

1. "Aetna Reports Fourth Quarter and Full-Year 2004 Results." Available: http://www.aetna.com/news/2005/pr_4thquarter2004_earnings.htm.
2. "Aetna History." Available: http://www.aetna.com/history/index.htm.
3. E-mail communication with Donna Richmond, Security Advisor, Information Security Policy and Practices, Aetna, February 25, 2005.

4. From 1993 to 1994, Aetna issued a number of information security policies, standards, and procedures. In 1998, they were consolidated into a single Information Security Statement of Policy, which was signed by the Chairman and the CIO.

5. Donna Richmond, "Tips, Tricks & Techniques of a Successful Security Awareness Program," presented at the InfraGard Connecticut quarterly meeting, February 2, 2005.

6. Personal communication with Donna Richmond, Security Advisor, Information Security Policy and Practices, Aetna, February 9, 2005.

CASE STUDY QUESTIONS

1. Many organizations have tried, but have not been able, to implement a successful information security awareness program. How was Aetna able to succeed with its program?

2. Most companies tend not to fund security awareness programs during financially difficult times. When Aetna implemented its first InfoSec exam in 1999, the company's stock price was $99.87 per share. By February 2000, Aetna's stock price had fallen to $40.75. Despite rising costs and declining profits, the company continued to support its internal security awareness program. What reasons might Aetna have had for doing this?

3. The ISPP group consists of only five employees. Each year, they design, develop, and implement a new version of the InfoSec exam for more than 27,000 Aetna employees. Explain how this small group has been able to accomplish such a task.

4. Most of the eight to ten users who are selected for usability testing have an entry-level understanding of computers and tend to be uncomfortable with Web-based applications. Why aren't more experienced users chosen for testing?

5. Research at least five security awareness solution providers. Summarize their similarities and differences.

6. Why is it important for a company's officers to be able to demonstrate due care? How is due care related to negligence?

7. Beginning in 2003, the InfoSec exam became integrated within Aetna's Business Conduct and Integrity training program. What are the advantages of doing this? What are the disadvantages?

8. Why is it considered good practice for an organization to have its users officially sign off on its security policy?

9. What factors should be considered in the development of any information security awareness program?

10. It is often difficult to cost-justify an information security awareness program. What quantitative and qualitative factors should be considered when justifying the program's expense?

KEY TERMS

Access Control: Policies and mechanisms that restrict user access to computer resources.

Authorization: Following user authentication, the user is allowed access to system resources based on the user's identity.

Availability: Ensuring that information is accessible to authorized parties.

Business Continuity Plan: Strategy to minimize the effect of a disruptive event and to allow for the resumption of critical business processes.

Computer Security Institute (CSI): Organization that has provided security education to information, computer, and network security professionals since 1974. Its Web site is http://www.gocsi.com.

Confidentiality: Preventing the unauthorized disclosure of information.

Disaster Recovery Plan: Comprehensive statement of actions for responding to an emergency. Provides the capability to implement critical processes at an alternative site and to return to normal operations within a satisfactory time frame.

Due Care: Center of corporate legal responsibility. Concerns the ability to foresee damage, the connection between the corporation's conduct and the damage, the amount of damage incurred, the blame that can be attached to the corporation's conduct, and the corporation's policy of preventing future damage.

Health Insurance Portability and Accountability Act (HIPAA): Information privacy law sponsored by Senators Kennedy and Kassenbaum and passed in 1996. Calls for appropriate administrative, technical, and physical controls to protect the privacy of individual health information.

Information Security (InfoSec): Protecting information against unauthorized disclosure, transfer, modification, or destruction.

Integrity: Preventing the unauthorized modification or destruction of information.

SANS Institute: Cooperative research and education organization established in 1989. SANS stands for SysAdmin, Audit, Network, Security. Its Web site is http://www.sans.org/.

Security Policy: High-level statement of the organization's security rules and practices. The security policy regulates how the organization manages, protects, and distributes sensitive information.

User Authentication: Process that verifies the identity of an individual. Ensures that the user is who she or he claims to be.

INDEX